Allen Sweeny

ROI Basics
for
Nonfinancial
Executives

A Division of American Management Associations

Library of Congress Cataloging in Publication Data

Sweeny, Allen.
  ROI basics for nonfinancial executives.

  Includes index.
  1. Capital investments—Evaluation. I. Title.
HG4028.C4S95   658.1'527   79-17296
ISBN 0-8144-5553-0

First Printing

To
Manna and Pappy

Author's Note

Basics, by definition, should address not only what is first but also what is essential. Certainly this short book on ROI basics has been written with this intent and is directed at the nonfinancial executive who has no prior knowledge of ROI concepts or techniques. It is hoped that the ten short chapters that follow will provide a readable solution to that problem.

I want to particularly thank Cathy Coult for her significant editorial as well as conceptual contributions to this book. She was instrumental in finally bringing it to completion. My thanks also to Donna Bozzella for her patient, cheerful, and competent assistance in so many ways and particularly in the preparation of this manuscript.

Contents

1

Return on Investment: The Concept and Its Importance

Rᴇᴛᴜʀɴ on investment analysis, frequently referred to as ROI, is highly touted as a modern managerial technique. The words evoke images of pages of mathematical formulas and complex calculations. Surely this technique is the product of twentieth century wizardry—computerized of course.

But the basic concept underlying return on investment— that capital is entitled to a return for its use—is almost as old as the use of money itself. In classical Greece, wealthy individuals loaned money to others for a return, and "money changers" were a familiar sight in Biblical times.

Throughout the centuries, society has recognized that one is entitled to a return for the wise use of his money. In the early 1800s, the English economist David Ricardo used this concept in his systematization of economics, laying the groundwork for modern economic systems. Ricardo defined the three basic factors of production as land, labor, and capital. Each element, said Ricardo, is entitled to a return for its use: The return on land for its contribution to the economic process is rent; the return on labor is wages; and the return on capital is interest.

This centuries-old concept is the backbone of our "modern" technique. And just as the basic concept underlying return on investment is not truly modern, neither is it complex. A good way to demonstrate the basic simplicity of the ROI concept is to use an example familiar to all of us—the bank loan.

When a bank makes a loan, it is entitled, according to economic theory, to a return on its capital—its investment. This return is the interest you pay on the loan.

Let's assume you borrow $1,000 from your local bank at 8% interest. You agree to pay back the loan plus interest in five annual installments of $250 each. Your annual $250 payment includes a repayment of the bank's investment, or principal, and the interest—a return to the bank for the use of its money during the year. When the bank receives your payment each year, it deducts the interest charges; the remainder of the payment is used to repay the principal.

Table 1 shows how each annual payment is divided into repayment of principal and of interest. At the end of the first year, the bank calculates the amount of interest due at 8%—a total of $80. When this amount is deducted from your first $250 annual payment, $170 remains to reduce the original investment, so that at the end of the first year the balance outstanding on the principal of the loan is $830.

At the end of the second year, you make another payment of $250. Once again the bank deducts its return on investment and applies the balance of the payment ($184) to reducing the principal. The same procedure is followed for the remaining three payments. Finally, by the end of the fifth year, you will have repaid the amount of the loan and your banker will have received a return of 8% on the principal outstanding at the end of each of the five years.

Table 1. Five annual payments of $250 on investment of $1,000.

Year	Annual Payment	Return of 8% on Investment at End of Year	Repayment of Principal	Bank's Investment at End of Year
0	—	—	—	$1,000
1	$250	$80	$170	830
2	250	66	184	646
3	250	52	198	448
4	250	36	214	234
5	250	19	231	3

We can see from this example that return is nothing more than the income that lenders or investors receive on funds they have either loaned or invested.

But even though the basic concept of return on investment is an old and simple one, its importance to modern business has never been greater. The chief executive of a highly capital-intensive company recognized the importance of ROI in his recent remarks: "Everyone recognizes that the name of the game is changing, and that the rules of the game are changing. But the fact that the scoring of the game must also change hasn't dawned on many people yet." By "scoring," he means the way we measure a company's success. We have traditionally used earnings per share for this measure, but return on investment is now more relevant and timely.

William Hawlett, president of Consolidated Foods, has

suggested pretty much the same thing. He feels that we should think of "profit" not in the conventional sense of net income, but as an acronym for the phrase "Proper Return On Funds Invested Today".

The growing recognition of the importance of return on investment is prompted by the convergence of a number of forces that promise to produce a radical and permanent restructuring of the basic economic system of the United States and of other industrialized nations. These forces are rapid inflation and a growing scarcity of capital.

In the last chapter of this book we will discuss the importance of ROI in the face of these other related new economic forces. For the moment, let's take a more simplified—but specific—situation to demonstrate the importance of return on investment to a business. Our case is that of Joe Smith and his widget machine tool shop. For years Joe Smith has dreamed of having his own widget shop. He's worked long and hard as a machinist in a local foundry, and has accumulated some $50,000 in savings. When he unexpectedly inherits $25,000, he decides that the time is right to go ahead with his plan.

Joe plans to set up his business in a nearby garage that he rents. He anticipates that by paying himself the same salary he earned at the foundry and by hiring an assistant, he'll be able to make and sell enough widgets during his first year of operation to make a minimum net profit of $7,500. Joe's no financial genius, but he knows that if he can make a net profit of $7,500 on his investment of $75,000, he'll have a 10% return on his investment. (Subsequent chapters will detail various methods for calculating return on investment, but for the moment, let us assume that the basic formula is **net income ÷ net investment**.) Ten percent is not a sensational return, but it is certainly better than the 6% his money has been earning at the savings bank, and now that he has his own business, he'll have the opportunity to do even better in the years ahead.

With these thoughts in mind, Joe moves ahead. He purchases the necessary machinery and raw materials, and arranges with the local agent for the sale of his widgets. As he begins business, he has a total of $75,000 invested in "Joe's Widget Company."

Joe loves being in business for himself, but there's a catch: Unfortunately his sales forecasting was not as accurate as it should have been. To his chagrin, Joe discovers that in a nearby community a competitor has also begun manufacturing widgets—slightly superior widgets, in fact—so that Joe's sales are less than he anticipated. Thus, at the end of the first year, he finds that instead of earning the $7,500 net income he had anticipated, he has earned only $3,000. But he's still in the black, and even though his return is only 4%, he feels that if he were to change sales agents he would do better the following year.

But another year goes by, and his sales don't improve. In fact, Joe finds that at the end of the second year of operation, he has just broken even—he has earned no return on his investment.

Upon investigation, he finds that the only way he can manufacture widgets that compete with those of his competitor is to modify his manufacturing process. The modification will require the investment of an additional $50,000 in another machine. The problem, of course, is that Joe doesn't have $50,000—he's earned next to nothing from his business and he has totally exhausted his personal savings. So he consults several of his local bankers. All of them are reluctant to lend Joe the $50,000, pointing out that, in the face of competition, he is unlikely to be able to earn the 8% interest ($4,000) they feel they would have to charge him on a loan of $50,000.

In desperation Joe decides to call upon his wealthy Uncle Luke, who has a sizable fortune and is reputed to be an astute businessman. Joe presents Uncle Luke with his problem and his plan to salvage his widget enterprise. Uncle Luke is sympathetic and listens patiently to his nephew's plight, but his response shows that his reputation for business savvy is well deserved. "Look Joe," he says. "I'd like to help, but it really doesn't make sense. I'm afraid we'd be throwing good money after bad. Your historical and prospective return on this business is below your cost of capital—the 8% that the bankers will charge you for a loan. As you know, they'd normally charge about 7 percent. The fact that they want 8% shows their concern about the riskiness of your proposal. I could make a stock investment in your business, but the return I would receive is considerably less than what I can expect from many alternative investments. So my investing in your business doesn't make any sense for me. And as for you, you are earning less than you did when you had the funds invested in a savings account. What's more, you're earning less than this year's rate of inflation—7% to 8%. I honestly think you'd be better off letting it go."

Joe is confronted with a dilemma—he must find capital somewhere or lose both his dream and probably a good part of his original $75,000 investment. But if Uncle Luke won't invest in his business, who will?

Let's leave Joe here. The resolution of his problem is not nearly as important to us as are the conclusions we can draw from his experience. Joe's experience is common to all businesses, no matter what their size or their purpose, when they do not generate enough return on their investment to meet their cost of capital and to avoid decapitalization through inflation. Thus, any company that earns an inadequate return on investment, as Joe's did, finds:

1. Reinvestment growth is slowed. (Joe couldn't buy the new machine he desperately needed.)

2. Opportunities for expansion are limited. (Joe would have had to have a much higher return before he could even consider expanding his business.)

3. In the case of a publicly owned corporation, the return to the owners is reduced. (Uncle Luke wouldn't invest in Joe's business, because his return would have been too low.)

4. All the above factors combine to make the business's rate of return less competitive, which in turn increases the difficulty the business has in competing for the capital it needs. Thus, even if capital is available at all (and for Joe, it wasn't), the business will have to pay a higher price for it. As a result, a vicious cycle is established: As the return on existing capital deteriorates, the cost of new capital—the basic cost that any business must cover—continues to increase.

As simple as it sounds, Joe's story demonstrates what happens when a business cannot meet its cost of capital. It also demonstrates two additional points of obvious, but great, importance:

1. The prospective return on a new investment must be assessed accurately.

2. Once the investment is made and becomes an existing part of the business, it must continue to sustain an adequate return.

Joe's miscalculation of his first-year return cost him dearly. If he had had better information, he might have decided against making the investment or he might have considered an alternative. If Joe had been able to earn a higher rate of return once he had gotten the business started, he would not have had such difficulty in maintaining the business and in attracting the capital he needed to continue.

The failure of Joe's widget company, the classical concept of return on capital, and the increasing concern about the capital crunch of the 1980s, all bring us to the basic purpose of this book, which is to examine the concept of return on investment; to understand it; to see how it works; and to learn how it can be used as a managerial tool in evaluating new investments and in measuring the adequacy of return on investment in an existing business.

2

ROI Analysis of
New Investments:
Some Basic
Considerations

TWENTY centuries ago, Aristotle pointed out that "the first step is what counts." To end well, one must be begin well. This concept is nowhere more true than in the investment decision-making process. The success or failure of a new investment is determined to a large extent by the accuracy with which it is initially assessed. To put it another way, it is much easier to maintain an adequate ROI on a going business when the initial investments were sound and profitable. For this reason, techniques for the evaluation and analysis of return on new investments are vitally important and will necessarily be the primary focus of this book. First, however, a few brief comments on some more general considerations in the ROI analysis of new investments.

The Basic Investment Decision Rule

The basic question that should be asked about any new investment is: Is the investment justified by the earnings or savings it will create over its life? The techniques of ROI analysis, which we will explore in subsequent chapters, are tools used by management to quantify and evaluate the answer to this question. For the moment, let's confine ourselves to some general comments.

We should first recognize that the question of whether an investment is justified by the earnings or savings it will create over its life cannot be answered for all investments. Some investments do not have tangible incentives—such as savings or earnings—that can justify them. The construction of an employees' lunchroom or a waste-treatment facility may be one of the most important investments a business makes for its future, but the benefits of either of these investments cannot be quantified. So, for investments of this kind, we have to rephrase our question: Is the investment justified by the *anticipated* benefits it will create over its life?

More frequently, however, the benefits associated with a particular investment are tangible and can be measured reasonably accurately. For these investments, as was pointed out, our first consideration is whether the investment can be economically justified. Let's use a simple example to illustrate the concepts and approaches involved in developing a rational answer to this question.

Suppose you have $5,000 in the bank in a 90-day time-deposit account and you are receiving interest at an annual rate of 7% ($300 per year). Let us also assume that you don't have a car and you rely exclusively on public transportation or, on occasion, car rentals. It occurs to you that you might be able to reduce your transportation costs if you had a car—not to mention the convenience of having permanent personal transportation at your disposal. You're willing to take your $5,000 out of the bank and to invest it in an economy model, but *only if* it is justified by the savings that you can obtain.

As a first step you begin to analyze what your average annual transportation costs have been over the last few years, and you find that they are as follows:

Public transportation to and from work	$ 300.00
Taxicabs for special occasions	200.00
Car rentals for weekend trips (about eight per year)	800.00
Car rental (annual two-week vacation)	800.00
Total costs	$2,100.00

The next step is to estimate what your annual transportation costs would be if you had your own car. First there would be automobile collision and liability insurance which would cost $300 per year. Gas, oil, and lubrication is the major cash expense in operating a car and these you calculate will amount to $400 per year based on annual average mileage of 8,000. (Estimated total mileage of 8,000 divided by an average of 20 miles per gallon equals 400 gallons at 70¢ per gallon, for a total of $280. Oil and lubrication would be approximately another $100. The $400 annual cost at 8,000 miles per year works out to 5¢ per mile, which seems in line with accepted statistics on car operating costs.)

Maintenance and repairs are also costs that must be anticipated, even though the exact timing and amounts of these costs may be difficult to determine. General statistics indicate that they approximate 2¢ a mile—so estimate that they'll amount to $200 per year.

Finally you've got to take into account depreciation—or the annual reduction in the value of your automobile as the result of usage—and styling obsolescence. Since you'll be buying a compact, economy-sized automobile, styling obsolescence won't be as important a factor as it might otherwise be, but you will still need to plan on at least a $700 depreciation factor in the first few years of ownership.

In summary, the various costs of car ownership are estimated to total $1,600 per year as summarized here:

Insurance	$ 300.00
Gas and oil	400.00
Maintenance	200.00
Depreciation	700.00
Total	$1,600.00

This $1,600 per year of estimated expenses is obviously $500 less than the $2,100 that you calculate you now spend on transportation. What's more, this saving is greater than the $350 of annual interest that you now receive on the $5,000 that you have in your savings account (and that you would use to purchase the car).

You don't have to be a financial genius to recognize that the $500 per year that you will save by owning a car is greater than the $350 a year you earn as interest on your savings in the bank. And you'll have the additional convenience of actually owning a car.

But there's still another consideration: You must pay federal income taxes on the interest you receive from the bank. Assume that you are in a 30 percent tax bracket. Thus, the government will take $105 of the interest you receive in taxes, leaving you with a net *after-tax* income of $245. The $500 you estimate you'll save by owning your own car isn't similarly taxed, since it is a personal economy. So, when you consider your tax situation, the incentive for an automobile purchase looks even more attractive—a $500 saving both before and after taxes compared with $350 of interest income before tax and $245 after.

If your estimates and assumptions are realistic, you can logically conclude that you *should* buy the car. The investment appears to be a good one, and seems justified by the savings it will create. Although this simple example ignores many of the nuances and finer points of investment analysis (to which we will turn in subsequent chapters), it nonetheless illustrates the basic steps involved in any new investment analysis, no matter how complex. These basic steps can be summarized as follows:

1. Identify and quantify the amount of the investment (in our case, the car).

2. Determine the savings—or in some cases, the earnings—that will result from the investment. (In our case, we concluded that by owning a car we could save $500 per year *before taxes.*)

3. Identify the effect of tax costs on the new savings or earnings that you expect from the investment. (In our case, the savings from car ownership was even more attractive because it was not taxed vis-à-vis the alternative interest income that we could receive.) In some cases, tax consequences can also affect our investment, as in the case of tax investment credits or other such devices. We will discuss this in greater detail later.

4. Determine if the investment is justified by the savings or earnings or by some of the intangible benefits it will create. (In our case, the tangible savings both before and after taxes justified the investment vis-à-vis the alternative of a savings account. Additionally, there was the intangible benefit of having your own car).

In principle, the basic steps in the investment process appear simple; in actual application, however, they can often become more complex. Let's take a few examples to illustrate the point.

We've said that the first step in any analysis of an investment is to identify the amount of the investment itself. What could be more simple? All we need to know is the cost of the machinery or equipment (and the costs involved in delivery and installation) in which we want to invest. In our case, it was the cost of a new car. But now let's assume that after we have owned the car for a few months we find we must build a garage to house it. Obviously, the cost of building a garage greatly increases the amount of our investment. It's certain that the savings of $500 that we expected will not justify the investment of the car and a new garage. Because we overlooked the necessity of investing in a garage, we no longer have a good investment.

As absurd as the oversight in our example may seem, the problem of accurately assessing the real magnitude of any new investment is not always that easy. For example, is the investment in a new petroleum refinery only the cost of the refinery itself? What about the service stations that may need to be built to sell the gasoline? Or the trucks, the pipelines, and the tankers to transport the crude oil? This illustrates an important point: You can't determine whether savings or earnings will justify an investment until you're sure how much that investment will be.

The second step in investment analysis calls for a determination of the net savings, earnings, or benefits. Here again, the simplicity of this principle may be misleading. In our car purchase analysis, the $500 that we calculated we could save by owning a car included $800 that was spent on car rental during our annual two-week vacation. But let's assume that independently of our decision to buy the car, we decide that our annual vacation is an extravagance that we can no longer afford and that we will take our vacation away every other year rather than annually. The car rental expenses of $800 a year will now be reduced to $400. As a result of this decision, $400 of savings that were ascribed to the investment (the purchase of the car) are no longer directly related to the investment itself; they are the result of a totally independent decision—whether to take a vacation away from home each year.

On the basis of these examples, we can make two fundamental observations about ROI analysis. The first and most important is that ROI analysis—no matter how extensive, complex, or sophisticated—is *no better than the basic assumptions* used in determining the amount of the investment and the anticipated earnings or savings. The second, closely related to the first, is that any accurate ROI assessment can include only those costs that are truly, objectively relevant to the investment decision being evaluated. As obvious as these simple points may seem, "relevant economics" and "realistic assumptions" are the sine qua non of any intelligent, objective analysis of a new investment.

To begin well is to end well. Our analysis of the financial justification for purchasing a car has demonstrated the importance of correctly identifying and assessing the new investment. But in making any major investment decision, a business must consider something else as well—the future.

The capital investment decision is a kind of monument to the future. A new investment usually involves significant expenditures for property, plant, and equipment, the "fixed assets" the business will use to produce its goods and services. Should the investment prove to be unprofitable, these assets are not easily disposed of. Furthermore, associated with the fixed assets are certain "fixed costs"—costs that do not vary regardless of the profitability of the investment.

"Depreciation" is a good example of a fixed cost. (Depreciation, as you probably know, is the process of charging the estimated use, or deterioration, of an asset as an expense against the business.) Depreciation is charged over the useful life of an asset, usually from 10 to 25 years for machinery and 25 years or more for buildings.

Let's assume a manufacturer has invested $1,000,000 in a machine that has a useful life of 10 years. By using the "straight-line" method of depreciation (one of three methods he may use), the manufacturer charges his business $100,000 a year over the 10-year period.

But let's suppose that after the fourth year of the machine's operation the country's economy takes a sharp downturn and profits for all businesses sag. The manufacturer is hooked with those $100,000 yearly depreciation charges for another six years, an expense he may no longer be able to afford because of his declining income. He may decide he has to sell the machine, something that would be very difficult to do in a recessionary period. If he is lucky enough to find a buyer he will undoubtedly sell the machine for a fraction of what it was worth. A bad investment is almost always a bargain for the buyer at the expense of the original investor. To grasp this point, one need only recollect that major U. S. corporations wrote off millions of dollars in the last few years as they owned up to the investments that they had made during the Soaring Sixties but that had gone sour in the 1970s.

The permanence of the capital investment decision distinguishes it from other types of business decisions. To make this distinction clear, let's consider another kind of investment decision—the decision to undertake a 10-year sales expansion of a product. The cost of the expansion is estimated at $1,000,000, and the yearly cost will be (like the depreciation charge on the machine) $100,000. But if this company were to run into bad times and its profits were to decline, all it would have to do is to reduce or eliminate the program, since the company has no money tied up in expensive machinery or buildings and is therefore free to drop the sales program and use that $100,000 for other purposes.

Another aspect of the permanence of the capital investment decision is worth mentioning. Any capital investment decision is made within the context of a business strategy, and the impact of that decision on the total strategy should be thoroughly analyzed and evaluated before the decision is made. Once an investment decision is implemented, it binds the business to that strategy.

For example, consider the strategic implications of a decision to locate a new textile manufacturing plant in New England rather than in the South—or even in Taiwan or Mexico. In making this decision, the manufacturer must consider not only what type of textile should be manufactured and how much of it, but these other questions:

1. Is the labor supply adequate to meet present and anticipated needs?
2. What will be the current and estimated future labor costs, including benefits for employees?
3. How skilled is the labor force? How productive is it likely to be?
4. What are current and projected tax benefits or tax costs?
5. What are transportation costs for raw materials and finished products?
6. Are there any other advantages or disadvantages of investment in the United States as opposed to investment in foreign countries?

These are a few of the assessments that must be made concerning only a single aspect of the investment—the location of the new plant. The manufacturer will have to assess dozens of other factors by the time the final investment decision is made, and the company will have to live with the decision—either profitably or unprofitably—for a long, long time.

In these first two chapters we have looked at return on investment as a broad concept. We have stressed its importance and have discussed some of the basic steps in the analysis of a return on a new investment. Having established this groundwork, let us now examine more closely the three financial techniques that are used to quantify the return on a new investment.

3

The Basic Methods of Calculating ROI: The Payback and Accounting Methods

IN this chapter we will explore two of the three basic methods for quantifying the return on investment—the payback and accounting methods.

The Payback Method

As its name suggests, the payback method calculates the time it will take for a new investment to pay for itself. Like the method itself, the formula for calculating it is simple and straightforward:

$$\frac{\text{Original net investment}}{\text{Annual earnings after tax} + \text{depreciation}} = \text{payback period}$$

To demonstrate how the formula works, let's turn to another simplified example—John Brown, who is planning to buy a new machine for his own widget manufacturing business.

1. *Gross investment:* John has checked with several manufacturers and has received several bids. The machine best suited to his needs will cost $17,600. The cost of delivering and installing the machine on the factory floor will be $400. Thus, the total cost of the machine, including delivery and installation, is $18,000.

2. *Salvage value of old machine:* When the new machine is installed, John will retire his old machine, which he knows he can sell for $900.

3. *Savings relevant to new machine:* John wants to buy the new machine because it automates a step in the widget manufacturing process, thereby eliminating the services of one laborer. With the installation of the new machine, John will be able to save the wages and benefit costs for one employee, or $8,400.

4. *Other costs associated with the new machine:* The new machine will cost about the same as the old machine to operate, so there will be no difference in operating costs. The only additional costs will be the depreciation expense that was discussed in Chapter 2.

The first step in calculating depreciation is to estimate the useful life of the machine—let's say nine years. The second step is to estimate the machine's salvage value at the end of its useful life—let's say $1,800. The third step is to deduct the salvage value from the cost of the new machine. The remainder is the amount that must be depreciated over the life of the machine. Thus, when John deducts the estimated salvage value of $1,800 from the gross of $18,000, he will have $16,200 to be depreciated over the nine years of the machine's life.

Exhibit 1. Return On Investment: elements for payback calculation.

Gross Investment	
Cost of new machine	$17,600
Delivery and installation	400
Total gross investment	$18,000
Net Investment	
Gross investment	$18,000
Less salvage value for old machine	900
Total net investment	$17,100
Determination of Annual Depreciation Costs	
Gross investment in new machine	$18,000
Less estimated salvage value at end of useful life	1,800
Net investment to be depreciated	$16,200
Estimated life of machine	9 years
Annual depreciation expense based on straight-line depreciation method $16,200 ÷ 9 Years	$ 1,800
Savings as a Result of New Machine	
Elimination of one laborer's annual salary and benefits	$ 8,400

If he uses the straight-line method of depreciation (one of the three he could choose), John will have an annual depreciation cost of $1,800. (The annual depreciation charge on the straight-line method is calculated by dividing $16,200—the value to be depreciated—by the useful life of the machine—nine years.*

All these facts, which are summarized in Exhibit 1, provide John with the basic elements he needs to calculate the payback on his proposed investment.

In demonstrating how John calculates the payback on his

---

* For a further discussion of depreciation methods and the general concept of depreciation, please refer to Chapter 4 of my book *Accounting Fundamentals for Nonfinancial Executives* (New York: American Management Associations, 1972).

investment, we will follow the six steps (discussed in Chapter 2) that are basic to any investment decision.

IDENTIFY AND QUANTIFY INVESTMENT

Here we have two possibilities: We can choose to use either the net investment (cost of new machine less salvage value of the old machine) or the gross investment (cost of the new machine), although the particular choice between these two is not nearly as important as is the consistent use of that choice in subsequent investments. Therefore, if John uses his net investment in calculating the payback for this investment, he must use net investment in analyzing any future investments he makes.

John does in fact decide that net investment will produce a more accurate estimate of the investment's payback period. His net investment is $17,100 ($18,000–$900 salvage value for his old machine).

DETERMINE "NET" SAVINGS OR EARNINGS

The second step in basic investment analysis is to determine the annual savings or earnings generated by the investment and to identify any new costs associated with the investment. John's new machine generates savings (rather than earnings) and incurs depreciation costs of $1,800 a year.

Salary and benefit savings from elimination of one laborer	$8,400
Less annual depreciation costs associated with new machine	1,800
Net new savings before tax	$6,600

IDENTIFY TAX COSTS AND CONSEQUENCES

The third step is to determine the effect of income taxes on the net savings generated by the investment. If we assume that any new income or savings generated by John's business will be taxed at 48%, we can determine the tax effect on these savings as follows:

Salary and benefit savings from elimination of one laborer	$8,400
Less annual depreciation costs associated with new machine	1,800
Net new savings before tax	6,600
Federal income tax on new savings at 48%	3,168
Net new savings after tax	$3,432

Here it is necessary to say a few words about our tax calculations. First, we've used the 48% U.S. corporate tax rate on the increased earnings John anticipates as a result of his savings in labor. But if Brown Widget Enterprise earns less than $25,000 a year, its earnings would be taxed at a rate of 25%. Second, because depreciation is a tax-deductible expense, John's taxable savings are reduced by the amount of his depreciation expense. Thus, his gross savings ($8,400) less the depreciation costs of the new machine ($1,800) produces taxable savings of $6,600.

The denominator in the payback equation is the net annual profits after tax plus the annual depreciation. So, for Brown Widget, we have the following:

Net savings after tax	$3,432
Plus annual depreciation costs	1,800
Total	$5,232

Here again, some explanation is in order. As suggested by the term itself, payback refers to a time period in which an investment pays for itself, i.e., the investment generates enough cash to recover its original costs. As we have suggested in our earlier comments, the depreciation charges do not represent a cash outlay; they are only a bookkeeping adjustment to account for the cost incurred by using an asset over its life. This is why the annual depreciation charges are added back to the annual net profit.

Thus, in our example, John expects his investment to produce gross labor savings, or cash flows, of $8,400. We have calculated that John must pay $3,168 in taxes on these savings. This leaves him with $5,232 of net cash flow. We can get the same result by adding net savings after tax to annual depreciation cost, as is shown in Exhibit 2.

Exhibit 2. Determining cash flow (denominator for payback calculation).

Method I: Net After-Tax Savings plus Depreciation	
Net savings after tax	$3,432
Plus annual depreciation costs	1,800
Total annual cash flow	$5,232
Method II: Gross Cash Savings less Cash Tax Expense	
Gross cash labor savings	8,400
Less cash tax expense	3,168
Total annual cash flow	$5,232

We now have the denominator of our payback equation. Our next step is to obtain the numerator. In our example, this is simple—the numerator is simply the original net investment (the original cost of the machine, delivered and installed, less the salvage value of the old machine). Thus, the original net investment here is $17,100. The final step is simple division:

$$\frac{\text{Original net investment}}{\text{Annual earnings after tax} + \text{annual depreciation}} = \frac{\$17,100}{\$5,232} = 3.27$$

Since our denominator is expressed as *annual* earnings and *annual* depreciation, the result of our division can be expressed in years. So, we can say that the after-tax savings resulting from John's investment of $17,100 will pay back that investment in 3.27 years, about three years and three months.

INTERPRETATION AND EVALUATION

Without any great complexity, we have quantified the return on John's investment in terms of payback. As is true of most techniques in financial analysis, the mechanics are simple. Interpretation of the results, however, is what really counts. It's not difficult to calculate the payback period, but is three years and three months good or bad? And how does this information help John make a better investment decision?

A few thoughts come immediately to mind. First, we know that John has estimated that the machine will last nine years. So, if we calculate that the investment will be paid back in 3.27 years, the machine will contribute the savings it generates to John's cash flow for five years and nine months, nearly two thirds the useful life of the machine (9 years − 3.27 years = 5.73 years). On the basis of this, John can conclude that the machine is a sound investment.

But what if the increased cash flow generated by the investment is not so stable? What if, for example, John plans to invest in a new product line rather than a new machine, and his estimated increased cash flows will result from the sale of the new product rather than from savings in manpower? Earnings from new product sales are obviously much less certain than are the savings generated by the new machine. Savings usually are readily identified and controlled, but sales must be increased in the face of the uncertainties of the general economy and the actions of competitors. Thus, if John were investing in a new product, he probably would not be so confident about the payback period. He may desire a shorter payback, or he may simply be more cautious about making the investment.

In determining the adequacy of a payback period, we also need to take into account the nature of the industry in which the investment is being made. An electric public utility, for example, can predict with relative certainty what the future demand for electrical energy will be in the area it serves. The basic demand for electrical energy is well established, stable, and a necessity. Let us assume that the widget manufacturing industry has similar characteristics. Under this set of circumstances, three years and three months does not seem to be an unduly lengthy payback period. But what if John Brown were buying a machine to make a very special, high-fashion item of women's clothing. The fashion industry is "faddy" and "volatile," so that John might understandably conclude that a three-year, three-month payback was unacceptable.

How else might John use the payback method? If he were unhappy with his 3.27-year payback, he could look for other machines that might realize greater savings, perform payback calculations for each of these alternatives, and rank the machines according to their payback periods. This could help him decide which of the alternatives would produce the best return on his investment.

Finally, John might use the payback calculation to guide him in financing the investment. Let's suppose that he obtained a five-year loan for the purchase of the machine. In that case, the investment—with its three-year, three-month payback—would have already been repaid by the savings it had generated at the time the loan was due, and it would have contributed to business profits for almost two years. If the loan had been due in two years, however, then the investment would not have generated any savings to contribute to John's cash flow. Under those circumstances, to pay back the loan when it was due, John would have had to divert cash from other areas of his operations, and thereby possibly strain his business's financial resources.

Thus, the payback method. As an analytical technique, it is simple, direct, and practical. (Its advantages and limitations will be evaluated in Chapter 6.) But now let's look at the second basic method of calculating ROI—the accounting method.

The Accounting Method

The accounting method is another simple way to measure return on investment. To calculate the ROI by the accounting method, determine the net savings or earnings after depreciation and tax costs and divide that number by the total net investment, as in the following equation:

$$\frac{\text{Net savings (earnings) after depreciation and tax}}{\text{Net investment}} = \text{return on investment}$$

To demonstrate the use of the accounting method, let's turn again to John Brown's proposed purchase of a new widget machine that we used as the basis for our discussion of the payback method. The specific elements are the same and are summarized in Exhibit 3.

If we apply this information to our formula for quantifying ROI by the accounting method, we have:

$$\frac{\text{Net savings after tax}}{\text{Net investment}} = \frac{\$3,432}{\$17,100} = 20.1\%$$

Note that the numerator of the equation equals net savings after depreciation and taxes, or $3,432. In determining the numerator, depreciation costs are deducted from savings (as with the payback method) because depreciation is a tax-

Exhibit 3. Return On Investment: elements for accounting
method calculation.

Investment	
Gross Investment	
Cost of new machine	$17,600
Delivery and installation	400
Total gross investment	$18,000
Net Investment	
Gross investment	$18,000
Less salvage value for old machine	900
Total net investment	$17,100

deductible expense and reduces the amount of tax that must
be paid on the savings (or earnings) that result from the investment.

The denominator is net new investment, or $17,000.
When we perform the division in the formula, we determine
that the new investment will yield a return of 20.1%

INTERPRETATION AND EVALUATION

Once again, the problem is how to interpret this information. Exactly what does a 20.1% return on investment mean?
And how can John use this information to make a better decision?

As with the payback method, John can calculate ROI for
alternative investments and then rank them in order of the return they produce. All other things being equal, he could then
select the machine that would give him the highest return.

The return as determined under the accounting method
can also be compared directly with the return on investment
as we defined it in Chapter 1—the interest cost on a loan or
the interest yield on a savings deposit. Thus, for example,
John's 20.1% return on his investment in the machine is far

more attractive than the 6% or 7% he would earn if he kept this money in a time-deposit account. The difference, of course, is that the 6% to 7% return that John would earn from the savings deposit is a certainty, whereas the return on the investment in the machine depends on the continued success of John's business and the accuracy of his assumptions on the amount of labor he can save.

The rate of return as calculated under the accounting method can also be compared with the cost of the capital used to make the investment. If John must borrow money at 8% from the bank to purchase the machine, he knows that the cost of the capital used to purchase the machine will be amply covered by the anticipated ROI.

In Chapter 6, we will give a critical evaluation of the advantages and some of the shortcomings of the accounting method. But in the meantime, let's turn to the third and more complicated method of investment evaluation—present value analysis.

4

Present Value ROI Analysis: The Basic Concepts

THE present value methods of ROI analysis hinge on the basic reality that money has a "time value." This idea is neither new nor complex, but we can perhaps facilitate our understanding of the concept if at the outset we indulge in a bit of fantasy.

Assume that as you read these words you are interrupted by a phone call. When you answer, you learn that you have been chosen the winner in a promotion for the state government's new lottery. You can receive $5,000 cash immediately—or as an alternative, you can elect to be paid $7,500 five years from now. You have a day to decide how you prefer to receive your lucky winnings. Whether $5,000 today is better or worse than $7,500 five years from now can only be answered objectively if we consider the time value of money.

When we refer to the time value of money, we simply mean that it is usually better to receive a given amount of money sooner than later. Why? Because from the beginning of civilization, payment for the use of money has been in the form of interest. Thus, understanding the relationship between time and money (that is, the time value of money) begins with nothing more complicated than understanding an ordinary savings account. From our early childhoods— whether we are now business professionals, executives, stockholders, or bankers—we have all learned to compare our investment opportunities with the fundamental of all fundamentals: the compound interest rate return of a risk-free deposit in a savings account. Compound interest means interest paid on both the principal that we have deposited and the interest that accures on that principal, assuming that the interest income we receive is reinvested at the same rate of interest. This is something that once again we all know and take for granted in a regular savings account. Compound interest rates are used to determine the value of money over time. Thus, assume you have $1,000 and you leave it on deposit for a period of five years at an annual rate of interest of 10%, compounded annually. It will grow in value over time, as shown in Table 2.

Table 2. Growth of $1,000 at 10% annual compound rate of interest.

Year	Principal Plus Interest	Annual Interest at 10%	Amount at End of Year
1	$1,000.00	$100.00	$1,100.00
2	1,100.00	110.00	1,210.00
3	1,210.00	121.00	1,331.00
4	1,331.00	133.10	1,464.10
5	1,464.10	146.41	1,610.51

The $1,000 left on deposit at a compound annual interest rate of 10% will have grown to a total value of $1,610.51 at the end of five years. This consists of the original $1,000 of principal and $610.51 of interest.

We can see that it is a relatively easy matter to apply the simple mathematics of compounding to determine what money today will be worth in the future. Obviously, all we need to know is (a) What is the amount of money to be deposited today? (b) What annual (or perhaps semiannual) rate of interest will be used to compound the principal? (c) For how long (how many years or months) will the principal be left to earn the compound interest.

At this point, the reader should undoubtedly recognize that quantifying the time value of money through interest compounding, as we have just illustrated and discussed, also provides us with a mechanism to determine whether we want our fantasy lottery winnings to be $5,000 today or $7,500 five years from now. The procedures that we follow would be the same, and again we will make the assumption that our deposit, the principal, will earn a 10% compound annual rate of interest. The amount of principal is obviously the $5,000 that we have if we take our prize as an immediate cash payment. The value of this $5,000 in five years at a compound annual interest rate of 10% would be calculated as in Table 3.

Table 3. Value of $5,000 in five years at compound annual interest of 10%.

Year	Principal Plus Interest	Annual Interest at 10%	Amount at End of Year
1	$5,000.00	$500.00	$5,500.00
2	5,500.00	550.00	6,050.00
3	6,050.00	605.00	6,655.00
4	6,655.00	665.50	7,320.00
5	7,320.00	732.05	8,052.55

At 10% compound annual interest, $5,000 will grow to $8,052.55 at the end of five years! This is $552.52 more than we would have had if we had chosen the option of receiving the lottery prize of $7,500 at the end of five years. Thus, by taking into account the time value of money—in this instance, at a rate of 10% per year—we can conclude that we would be better off taking our lucky winning in the form of an immediate $5,000 cash payment.

Compound interest is the conceptual cornerstone of the time value of money, and it is the essence of present value analysis. In our use of the concept thus far, we have actually calculated the compound interest values that were relevant to our illustrations. As we have seen, this is simple enough to do; but it is hardly necessary, since precalculated compound interest calculations are readily available, and will be found in Appendix A of this book for interest factors up to 50% and for time periods up to 30 years. A sample is shown in Table 4.

Table 4. Compound interest tables for 1%–10% interest over 30 years.

Year	1%	2%	3%	4%	5%	6%	7%	8%	9%	10%
1	1.010	1.020	1.030	1.040	1.050	1.060	1.070	1.080	1.090	1.100
2	1.020	1.040	1.061	1.082	1.102	1.124	1.145	1.166	1.188	1.210
3	1.030	1.061	1.093	1.125	1.156	1.191	1.225	1.260	1.295	1.331
4	1.041	1.082	1.126	1.170	1.216	1.262	1.311	1.360	1.412	1.464
5	1.051	1.104	1.159	1.217	1.276	1.338	1.403	1.469	1.539	1.611
6	1.062	1.120	1.194	1.265	1.340	1.419	1.501	1.587	1.677	1.772
7	1.072	1.149	1.230	1.316	1.407	1.504	1.606	1.714	1.828	1.949
8	1.083	1.172	1.267	1.369	1.477	1.594	1.718	1.851	1.993	2.144
9	1.094	1.195	1.305	1.423	1.551	1.689	1.838	1.999	2.172	2.358
10	1.105	1.219	1.344	1.480	1.629	1.791	1.967	2.159	2.367	2.594
11	1.116	1.243	1.384	1.539	1.710	1.898	2.105	2.332	2.580	2.853
12	1.127	1.268	1.426	1.601	1.796	2.012	2.252	2.518	2.813	3.138
13	1.138	1.294	1.469	1.665	2.133	2.133	2.410	2.720	3.066	3.452
14	1.149	1.319	1.513	1.732	1.980	2.261	2.579	2.937	3.342	3.797
15	1.161	1.346	1.558	1.801	2.079	2.397	2.759	3.172	3.642	4.177
16	1.173	1.373	1.605	1.873	2.183	2.540	2.952	3.426	3.970	4.595
17	1.184	1.400	1.653	1.948	2.292	2.693	3.159	3.700	4.328	5.054
18	1.196	1.428	1.702	2.026	2.407	2.854	3.380	3.996	4.717	5.560
19	1.208	1.457	1.754	2.107	2.527	3.026	3.617	4.316	5.142	6.116
20	1.220	1.486	1.806	2.191	2.653	3.207	3.870	4.661	5.604	6.728
25	1.282	1.641	2.094	2.666	3.386	4.292	5.427	6.848	8.632	10.835
30	1.348	1.811	2.427	3.243	4.322	5.743	7.612	10.063	13.268	17.449

Note that the compound interest factors are expressed on the basis of $1.00 and can thus be readily multiplied by any given amount of money. For example, a shortcut to obtaining the value of $5,000 in five years at 10% is simply to refer to the table and look for the factor for 10% at the end of five years—which is 1.611. If we multiply this by $5,000.00 (1.611 x 5,000), we get a value of $8,055.

In our calculation we actually ended up with a figure of $8,052.55. The difference between this number and the $8,055 we obtained by using the compound interest factors is because the value of $1.00 at the end of five years at 10% actually compounds to $1.61051 (1.61051 × 5,000 = 8.052.55), but in the compound interest table, it is rounded off to the third digit—hence, $1.611.

Future Value vs. Present Value

We have seen how compounded interest can help us determine the *future* value of a *current* dollar. Thus, if we have $1.00 at present, we know that in five years at 10% compound interest it will become $1.611. At 8% interest it will become $1.469 at the end of five years. At 9% it will become $1.539 after five years. (See Table 4 or, for rates above 10%, refer to compound interest tables in Appendix A.)

But now let us turn the question around and ask how we can determine what money that we will receive in the *future* is worth to us *now*—or, in other words, what is the *present value* of money. Since we use compound interest factors to determine the "future value" of money we receive in the *present,* it is logical that they also be used to determine the *present value* of money that we will receive in the future. Let's be more specific. If we refer again to our compound interest table, we see that at 10% interest a dollar today will have the following values in the future:

Value today	$1.000
Value in 1 Year	1.100
Value in 2 Years	1.210
Value in 3 Years	1.331

With the above figures in front of us, let us ask again: If money is worth 10% to us, or if we can get a 10% return (interest) on it, what is the *present value* of a dollar that will be received a year from now? If at an interest rate of 10%, $1.00 received today will be worth $1.10 a year from now, then the value of $1.00 received a year from now must be the reciprocal of its "future value" of $1.10. The derivation of its "present value" at 10% would then be carried out as follows.

$$\frac{\text{Value today}}{\text{Value a year from now}^*} = \frac{\$1.00}{\$1.10} = .909 \ (\text{present-value reciprocal})$$

The same procedure would be used to determine the present value reciprocal at the end of the second and third years:

$$\frac{\text{Value today}}{\text{Value two years from now}^*} = \frac{\$1.00}{\$1.210} = .826$$

$$\frac{\text{Value today}}{\text{Value three years from now}^*} = \frac{\$1.00}{\$1.331} = .751$$

Let us review for a moment. Money has a time value because it is better to receive money sooner than later. Thus, as our illustration indicates, if money is worth 10% a year, the dollar we receive a year from now actually has a value of

---

* At compound interest rate of 10% per year.

only $0.909 to us right now. If we had the dollar now and could keep it for a year, we would increase its value by the interest factor (10%). Since we do not have it now—and must wait a year to receive it—we use the interest factor to decrease its value. Another way to express the idea is to say that we have "discounted" the value of the dollar that we will receive a year from now in order to reflect the fact that we do not have it now.

We can actually prove the validity of our "discounting" for the present value derivation in several ways.

As shown above, the present value of $1.00 at 10% interest received three years from now is $0.751. If this is true, then conversely we should be able to invest $0.751 today at a 10% compound interest rate and have $1.00 three years from now.

Year	Principal Plus Interest	Annual Interest at 10%	Amount at End of Year
1	$0.751000	0.075100	0.826100
2	0.826100	0.082610	0.908710
3	0.908710	0.090871	0.999581

Our $0.751 investment at 10% has grown to $0.999 or $1.00 at the end of the third year.

The validity of the discounting process can be seen from another perspective—namely, the absolute reciprocal relationship between compound interest factors and present value factors—or, as we have referred to them, present value derivations. This point is illustrated in the table at the top of the next page, using a 10% interest rate.

(Note: In general terms, "reciprocal" is defined as inversely related. The technical mathematical definition is "the quantity resulting from the division of 1 by the given quantity; a quantity which, when multiplied by the given quantity,

Time Period	Compound Interest Factor		Present Value Factor		Reciprocal
0	1.000	×	1.000	=	1
1	1.10	×	.909	=	1
2	1.21	×	.826	=	1
3	1.33	×	.751	=	1

equals 1. Example: the reciprocal of 7 is $1/7$''—Webster's *New World Dictionary*.)

We can see that discounting is reverse compounding. Indeed we can simply use a compound interest factor to calculate the reciprocal present value factor or derivation. Although these calculations may help demonstrate the relationship between these two concepts, such labor is necessary only for purposes of illustration. Precalculated present value tables are readily available, and are shown in Appendix B of this book at interest rates from 1% to 30% over period of 30 years. In Table 5, we can see that the factors for 10% are exactly the same as those we calculated.

The concepts and techniques of present value analysis allow us to quantify the benefit of money we expect to re-

Table 5. Present value table for 1–14% interest over 10 years.

Years	1%	2%	4%	6%	8%	10%	12%	14%
1	0.990	0.980	0.962	0.943	0.926	0.909	0.893	0.877
2	0.980	0.961	0.925	0.890	0.857	0.826	0.797	0.769
3	0.971	0.942	0.889	0.840	0.794	0.751	0.712	0.675
4	0.961	0.924	0.855	0.792	0.735	0.683	0.636	0.592
5	0.951	0.906	0.822	0.747	0.681	0.621	0.567	0.519
6	0.942	0.888	0.790	0.705	0.630	0.564	0.507	0.456
7	0.933	0.871	0.760	0.665	0.583	0.513	0.452	0.400
8	0.923	0.853	0.731	0.627	0.540	0.467	0.404	0.351
9	0.914	0.837	0.703	0.592	0.500	0.424	0.361	0.308
10	0.905	0.820	0.676	0.558	0.463	0.386	0.322	0.270

ceive in the future compared with the value of money today. This was our problem at the outset of the chapter—when we had to decide whether we wanted our prize to be $5,000 today or $7,500 five years from now. We were able to answer that question by taking into account the time value of money. We can obviously get the same answer by means of a present value analysis. Thus, the question becomes: If money is worth 10%, what is the present value of $7,500 received five years from now? To determine this, we look at our present value table and find that the present value of $1.00 received at the end of five years at 10% interest is $0.621. If $1.00 has a present value of $0.621, then the $7,500 we would expect to receive would be worth $4,657.50 (0.621 × $7,500 = $4,657.50). This $4,657.50 is less than the $5,000 we can receive as an immediate (*present*) cash prize. We should obviously opt for the $5,000 now.

Through the use of present value analysis, we were able to look at different amounts of money received at different times and to compare them. By way of further illustration, let us assume we were given the option to receive the $7,500 prize in five annual installments of $1,500 each: How would we feel about this alternative to a $5,000 immediate cash

Table 6. Calculating the present value of $7,500 paid in five installments of $1,500 each.

Time Period (Year)	Money Received	Present Value Factor at 10%	Present Value of Money Received
1	$1,500	0.909	$1,363.50
2	1,500	0.826	1,239.00
3	1,500	0.751	1,126.50
4	1,500	0.683	1,024.50
5	1,500	0.621	931.50
Total	$7,500		$5,685.00

payment? Once again, we would need to take into account the value of money, as in Table 6.

Under this alternative, our prize would have a present value of $5,685 and would thus be more valuable than $5,000, the present value of an immediate cash payment.

Obviously, understanding the time value of money and the techniques of quantity are important. They are always present in the various methods of determining present value ROI, which we will discuss in the next chapter.

5

Present Value
ROI Analysis:
The Basic Methods

THE principal difference between present value methods of ROI analysis and the accounting and payback methods is that the present value methods take into account the time value of money, which we discussed in the previous chapter. (Please note that when we speak of the "time value of money," we refer literally to cold, hard cash.) Thus, all methods of present value ROI analysis deal only with cash inflows or outflows associated with an investment. In addition, because present value methods take into account the value of money in relation to time, the cash inflows or outflows must be identified by a time period—that is, do they take place in the first, second, fifth, or eighth year of the investment project?

The first step in any ROI analysis is to identify the investment. With the present value methods, the investment must be identified in reference to cash and to when the investment takes place (one year, two years, or so on). The same thing is true in analyzing "savings" under present value methods. Savings, including tax effects, are only cash savings and must be identified by time period. Thus, if the cash savings are $3,000 for the first year and $2,000 for the second year, they should be recorded as such.

To illustrate these points more specifically, let us return to the investment/savings profile of Brown Widget Enterprise that we used in our illustrations for the payback and accounting ROI methods in Chapter 3. The elements for the ROI calculations that we used there are summarized in Exhibit 1.

The Cash Investment

Because we will use present value methods of ROI analysis, all these elements must be evaluated exclusively in terms of their cash impact. First let's look at our investment. The cost of the new machine is $17,600, and this will be paid for in cash. Therefore, it is a cash outflow. The delivery and installation cost must also be paid for in cash. Thus, we can identify a total of $18,000 of cash outflow associated with the gross investment. However, we also noted that John Brown expects to receive another cash payment of $900 for the salvage value of the old machine that is being replaced. This $900 reduces the total net investment to $17,100—the true cash outflow associated with the investment. Furthermore, we should note that all these cash outflows take place within essentially the same period of time and that they will be treated accordingly in our calculations. However, if in fact the investment were to be made over a period of two years, this would also have to be taken into account.

The Cash Savings

As a result of the investment in the new machine, we calculated that the net savings or net improvement after taxes to the profitability of John Brown's business would be as follows:

Salary and benefit savings from elimination of one laborer	$8,400
Less annual depreciation costs associated with new machine	1,800
Net new savings before tax	$6,600
Less federal income tax on new savings at 48%	3,168
Net new savings after tax	$3,432

The net new savings after tax have taken into account the effect of the annual depreciation costs that will result from the new machine. These depreciation expenses need to be considered in order to determine the effect of the investment on "net income or profit." However, as was noted in Chapter 3, depreciation is a cost that arises only from an accounting adjustment and *not* from a cash payment. Thus, the $3,432 of net new savings does *not* represent the cash savings that we must identify for our analysis with a present value method. This cash savings can be pinpointed—just as in the case of the payback method—by adding the $1,800 of "non-cash" depreciation charges to the $3,432 of net new savings. The result is as follows:

Net new savings after tax	$3,432
Plus annual depreciation costs	1,800
Total annual cash flows or earnings	$5,232

The reader will note that the annual cash flow or cash earnings of $5,232 represents the same number that we used in the denominator for our payback calculation in Chapter 3. You will recall that the payback method also seeks to isolate the "cash effect," since it attempts to determine how much cash will be generated in order to pay back the investment. Finally, we might also note that, as is almost always the case, federal income taxes on the new savings are assumed to be a cash expense associated with the investment. Here again, however, if this were not the case—that is, if for some reason these taxes could be deferred for payment in later years—this would also need to be taken into account in our present value analysis.

Earlier it was pointed out that in attempting to identify the cash elements in a present value ROI analysis, it is often useful to think in terms of "flows." Cash almost always flows out to make the investment, and subsequently flows in as a result of the net new savings or earnings. But there is one particular element of cash flow which merits special attention in present value analysis: residual-income cash flows.

Residual Income Cash Flows

The total gross investment in the new widget-forming machine, including installation, is $18,000. However, because we received $900 as scrap value for the old machine, our net investment was reduced to $17,100. Almost without exception, used equipment or machinery can be disposed of for some value. For this same reason when we calculated the total cost of the new machine that we have to depreciate over its expected useful life of nine years, it, too, had a salvage value. We assumed that this salvage value would be

$1,800, and accordingly reduced our original $18,000 cost to $16,200.

The economic fact of life that almost all assets have some terminal or residual value at the end of their useful lives is recognized in computing depreciation costs and also in all present value methods of ROI analysis. This is called "the residual value assumption," which is nothing more than an assumption about what cash payment can be expected for an asset at the end of that asset's useful life. As a general approach, the residual value of an asset is generally assumed to be the same as its expected final salvage value (although we should note that in today's highly inflationary economy, the tendency for tangible property to appreciate or hold its value has perhaps made this rather simplistic and conventional approach somewhat anachronistic). Under this method, the "residual value assumption" for the widget-forming machine would be the $1,800 that we have estimated as its salvage value. As we will see in subsequent illustrations, this residual value is assumed to be a cash inflow at the end of the investment's or project's economic life.

With these general points in mind, we can now examine the first of three basic methods of present value ROI analysis which (not surprisingly) is called the present value method.

The Present Value Method

Under this method, an investment proposal is acceptable if, apart from nonmonetary considerations, the present value of cash earnings at the desired rate of return is greater than or equal to the investment that is being made to generate the savings or earnings. The procedures for developing the computation to determine whether an investment is acceptable under the present value method can be summarized as follows:

1. Estimate the future cash outflows and inflows associated with the capital investment proposal for each specific year of the project's or investment's expected life.

2. Determine the rate of return desired for the project. (In Chapter 8, we will explore the various approaches to selecting such a rate; but for illustrative purposes, we will choose arbitrary rates in the following examples.)

3. Refer to the present value tables (Appendix B) to choose the correct present value factors under the rate of return that has been selected. Note that different present value factors will be required for each year.

4. Calculate the present value of the cash inflows (savings) for each year by multiplying them by the present value factors for that year.

5. Add up the total amount of the present value of each year's inflow for the life of the project. If the amount equals or exceeds the amount of the investment, that investment will be acceptable. If the sum of the net present value of the cash flows for each year is less than the amount of the investment, the investment will be unacceptable.

6. Bear in mind that nonmonetary considerations have been ignored. Make certain it is safe to do this. Also recognize that the validity of all these sophisticated calculations is no more accurate than the assumptions that underlie the estimates of investment or savings.

Now let us turn to an actual application of these procedures, again using our illustration of the investment in the widget-forming machine. The elements of our ROI analysis for this project under the present value method are set forth in Exhibit 4.

According to the procedures that we outlined above, the investment analysis under the present value method at our arbitrarily designated 20% rate of return appears in Table 7.

We can see that the total present value of all the cash sav-

Table 7. Calculation by present value method of ROI in widget-forming machine (desired rate of return, 20%).

Year	Item	Cash-Flow Effect Outflows/Inflows (dollars)		Present Value Factor at 20%		Present Value of Investments Outflows (dollars)	Present Value of Cash Flows, Savings, Inflows (dollars)
	Investment	(17,100)	×	1.000	=	(17,100)	
1	Cash savings	5,232	×	0.833	=		4,358
2	Cash savings	5,232	×	0.694	=		3,631
3	Cash savings	5,232	×	0.579	=		3,029
4	Cash savings	5,232	×	0.482	=		2,522
5	Cash savings	5,232	×	0.402	=		2,103
6	Cash savings	5,232	×	0.335	=		1,753
7	Cash savings	5,232	×	0.279	=		1,460
8	Cash savings	5,232	×	0.233	=		1,219
9	Cash savings	5,232	×	0.194	=		1,015
	Assumed cash residual value	1,800	×	0.194	=		349
Totals:	Investment					(17,100)	
	Savings						21,439

Exhibit 4. Elements of ROI calculation—present value method.

Investment (Outflows)	
Cost of new machine—cash outflow	$17,600
Delivery and installation—cash outflow	400
Total gross investment—cash outflow	$18,000
Less salvage value of old machine—cash inflow	900
Total net investment—net cash outflow	$17,100
Cash Savings (Inflows)	
Net new savings after tax	$3,432
Plus annual non-cash depreciation costs	1,800
Total annual cash savings (inflows)	$5,232
Estimated Project Life (same as estimated life of machine)	9 years
Residual Value	
Assumed to be estimated salvage value at end of machine's useful life (same as for depreciation calculation)—Cash inflow in ninth year	$1,800
Desired Earnings Rate (arbitrary figure)	20%

ings (inflows) that are assumed for nine years, including the assumed cash residual value, amounts to $21,439, which is $4,339 greater than the amount of our cash investment of $17,100. Therefore, under our present value decision rule, we can conclude that the investment is justified, since the present value of the savings (the cash inflows) exceeds the cash outflows associated with the investment, at the desired rate of return of 20%. By contrast, let us now follow exactly the same procedures, but in this instance we will set our desired rate of return at 30%. At this earnings rate, our present value analysis would result in the figures shown in Table 8.

As the calculations indicate, the expected cash savings or cash inflows, discounted at a present value factor of 30%, give a total present value of $15,959, which is $1,141 less

Table 8. Calculation by present value method of ROI in widget-forming machine (desired rate of return, 30%).

Year	Item	Cash Flow Effect Outflows/Inflows (dollars)		Present Value Factor at 30%		Present Value of Investments Outflows (dollars)	Present Value of Cash Flows, Savings, Inflows (dollars)
	Investment	(17,100)	×	1.000	=	(17,100)	
1	Cash savings	5,232	×	0.769	=		4,023
2	Cash savings	5,232	×	0.592	=		3,097
3	Cash savings	5,232	×	0.455	=		2,381
4	Cash savings	5,232	×	0.350	=		1,831
5	Cash savings	5,232	×	0.269	=		1,407
6	Cash savings	5,232	×	0.207	=		1,083
7	Cash savings	5,232	×	0.159	=		832
8	Cash savings	5,232	×	0.123	=		644
9	Cash savings	5,232	×	0.094	=		492
	Assumed cash residual value	1,800	×	0.094	=		169
Totals:	Investment					(17,100)	
	Savings						15,959

than the $17,100 investment. Therefore, under our present value decision rule, this project is unacceptable.

These two examples provide a useful illustration of (a) the application of the decision rule for the present value method in a positive as well as a negative situation; and (b) the mechanical procedures that are followed to arrive at the ROI calculation under the present value method. These two examples also usefully highlight the critical importance of the choice of the desired rate of return. We will discuss this aspect of the capital investment decision process in Chapter 8, but for the moment let us look at the second basic method of present value ROI analysis—the discounted cash flow or the internal rate of return method.

Discounted Cash Flow—Internal Rate of Return

Discounted cash flow and internal rate of return are two different names that are used for exactly the same method of ROI analysis. Discounted cash flow is also often expressed as the acronym "DCF." (A waggish student of ROI once suggested that the term more appropriately stood for "*D*on't *C*omprehend *F*ully," although it is hoped that the following discussion will refute this allegation.)

The basic difference between the present value method that we looked at earlier and the DCF–internal rate of return method is simply that under the DCF/IRR approach, the analyst has to find a present value factor that will *discount* the expected future outflows so that they will equal the investment, given the present value of money. The decision rule, therefore, for the DCF/IRR method can be stated as follows:

An investment proposal is acceptable if, apart from nonmonetary considerations, the present value of the cash earnings or inflow equals the

Table 9. Calculation of ROI in widget-forming machine (DCF/IRR method).

Year	Item	Cash Flow Effect (Outflow)/Inflow (in dollars)	Present Value Factor at 26%	Present Value of Cash Flows Investment Savings (in dollars) (Outflows)	Inflows	Cash Flow Effect (Outflow) Inflow (in dollars)	Present Value Factor at 28%	Present Value of Cash Flows Investment Savings (in dollars) (Outflows)	Inflows
	Investment	(17,100) ×	1.000	(17,100)		(17,100) ×	1.000	(17,100)	
1	Cash savings	5,232 ×	0.794		4,154	5,232 ×	0.781		4,086
2	Cash savings	5,232 ×	0.630		3,296	5,232 ×	0.610		3,192
3	Cash savings	5,232 ×	0.500		2,616	5,232 ×	0.477		2,496
4	Cash savings	5,232 ×	0.397		2,077	5,232 ×	0.373		1,952
5	Cash savings	5,232 ×	0.315		1,648	5,232 ×	0.291		1,523
6	Cash savings	5,232 ×	0.250		1,308	5,232 ×	0.227		1,188
7	Cash savings	5,232 ×	0.198		1,036	5,232 ×	0.178		931
8	Cash savings	5,232 ×	0.157		821	5,232 ×	0.139		727
9	Cash savings	5,232 ×	0.125		654	5,232 ×	0.108		565
	Assumed cash residual value	1,800 ×	0.125		225	1,800 ×	0.108		194
Totals:	Investment			17,100				17,100	
	Savings				17,835				16,854

investment at a present value factor—or a rate of return—that is considered acceptable.

Because under the DCF/IRR method a rate of return must be found and *then* a determination made as to whether it is acceptable, the procedures used in the computation vary greatly from those used in the present value method, and are as follows:

1. The estimated future net cash outflows and inflows to be derived from the capital investment proposal are identified year by year (Just as in the present value method).

2. A present value factor, which it is thought would discount the future cash savings (inflows) so that they will equal the investment, is estimated. (Note that there is no other way to approach this than to use a simple trial-and-error method.)

3. Once such an approximate present value factor has been identified, the next higher or lower present value factor should be used to discount the cash savings, following the same method. From these two "bridging" calculations, the exact rate that would make the cash savings equal the investment should be interpolated. (An explanation and illustration of this interpolation procedure follows shortly.)

To illustrate these procedures, we will again use our widget-forming example. All the elements for our ROI analysis are the same and the return on investment calculation under the DCF/IRR method would be as illustrated in Table 9.

PROCEDURE TO INTERPOLATE EXACT RETURN RATE
UNDER DCF/IRR METHOD

We want the exact rate (present value factor) that discounts cash savings to exactly $17,100 of investment. At a rate of 26%, cash savings discount to a total present value of $17,835. At 28%, cash savings discount to a total present value of $16,854. Therefore, the exact rate must be some-where between 26% and 28%, and the 2% difference between those two rates results in a $981 difference in the present value of the cash savings.

Present value cash savings at 26%	$17,835
Present value cash savings at 28%	16,854
Difference	$ 981

The difference between the amount of $17,100 to which we want to *exactly* discount and the total amount of the present value of the cash earnings at 26% is $735.

Present value cash savings at 26%	$17,835
Amount to which we want to exactly discount	17,100
Difference	$ 735

The ratio between these two is .75—735 divided by 981 equals 75%. Thus 75% of the 2% rate difference will give us the exact rate (present value factor) which will discount the cash savings to $17,100. This rate is 26% plus 1.5% (75% × 2%), or a total of 27.5%.

As we can see, the widget-forming machine has an estimate rate of return of 27.5%. This is the rate on the present value factor that discounted the future cash savings so that it equaled the investment. Since we have already said that a return of 20% is acceptable, the widget-forming machine with its 27.5% return meets this requirement and can be approved. Assume that we now insist upon a 30% return. Under this criterion, the project's expected 27.5% percentage return would *not* be acceptable, and the project would be rejected. Note again the importance that the choice of the desired rate of return has on the decision process—although in this case it occurred a step later than it did under the simple present value method.

Excess Present Value Index

Let us conclude by taking a brief look at one final variation on the use of present value ROI techniques—the excess present value (EPV) index. As we have discussed, the DCF/IRR method expresses ROI as a single percentage, and if that rate of return is found to be acceptable, the entire project will *then* be judged acceptable. In certain instances, the exclusive use of the DCF/IRR approach can lead to erroneous conclusions. When this is the case, the EPV indexing method is a useful supplementary tool.

Assume, for example, that we have an opportunity to invest in one, but only one, of two projects. Project A calls for an investment of $1,000 and has estimated cash earnings (including residual cash values) of $1,200 for one year. The present value factor which discounts this $1,200 back to the $1,000 of investment is $0.833 ($1,200 × 0.833 = $999.60 or $1,000), which would indicate a return of 20%.

Project B also calls for an investment of $1,000 and has estimated cash earnings (including residual cash values) of $300 per year for five years. As the calculations in Table 10 show, a present value factor of 15% is found to discount these cash earnings back to the investment of $1,000.

On the basis of the DCF/IRR method, Project A appears preferable since it supposedly has a return of 20% versus one of 15% for Project B. However, let us suppose that upon further consideration we conclude that a 10% rate of return is acceptable. The cash earnings for both projects are now discounted at this rate and would appear as in Table 11.

The next step, then, would be to employ the EPV Index, which would involve nothing more than indexing the two investments in terms of the relationship of the present value of the expected earnings to the investment at this 10% rate. As shown in Exhibit 5, Project A would have an EPV index of

Table 10. Project B: ROI calculation (DCF/IRR method).

Year	Item	Cash Flow Effect (Outflows)/ Inflows (in dollars)	Present Value Factor at 15%	Present Value of Cash Flows Investment/Savings (in dollars)	
	Investment	(1,000)		(1,000)	
1	Cash savings	300	0.870		261.00
2	Cash savings	300	0.756		227.00
3	Cash savings	300	0.658		197.40
4	Cash savings	300	0.572		171.60
5	Cash savings	300	0.497		149.10
Totals				1,000	1,006.10

Table 11. Comparison of cash earnings of Project A vs. Project B at 10% present value factor.

Year	Cash Savings (in dollars)	Present Value Factor at 10%	Present Value of Cash Earnings*
		Project A	
1	1,200.00	0.909	1,091
Total			1,091
		Project B	
1	300.00	0.909	273
2	300.00	0.826	248
3	300.00	0.751	225
4	300.00	0.683	205
5	300.00	0.621	186
Total			1,137

*Rounded to the nearest dollar.

1.09, whereas Project B would have an index of 1.14. Under such an index comparison, Project B would actually appear to be more attractive than Project A.

Exhibit 5. Excess present value index, Project A vs. Project B.

	EPV Index (excess present value of earnings/investment)
Project A Present value of $\dfrac{\text{cash earnings at 10\%}}{\text{Investment}} = \dfrac{\$1,091}{\$1,000}$	1.09
Project B Present value of $\dfrac{\text{cash earnings at 10\%}}{\text{Investment}} = \dfrac{\$1,137}{\$1,000}$	1.137

We can appreciate exactly the same point by recognizing that at the 10% discount factor, Project B will yield $1,137 of present value earnings, whereas Project A will yield only $1,091.

As the foregoing examples suggest, the excess present value index method is a useful supplementary analytical tool when alternative investments need to be compared in the face of limited funds available for investment.

6

Advantages and Limitations of the Various ROI Methods

In this chapter we will briefly review some of the advantages and limitations of the three basic ROI methods that we have now discussed.

The Payback Method

Undoubtedly, the strongest advantage of the payback method is its simplicity. It is quick and easy to calculate and not difficult to understand. For these reasons, it is an excellent but rough device for a preliminary screening of many capital investment proposals.

The payback method evaluates investments in terms of time (such as a payback of 3½ years), and this can be very useful where high technology, style, or economic risks are involved. Different industries also require different payback periods. For example, although a 10-year payback may be quite satisfactory to a public utility, it would probably be totally unacceptable to a computer manufacturer.

The payback method emphasizes cash recoverability of an investment, an emphasis that becomes more and more important as the cost of borrowing money constantly increases. Also, simply as a result of the methodology, the payback method gives weight only to those cash flows that occur at the beginning of the project. As we shall see later, this is also a limitation, but it is certainly in line with the general concept of the time value of money.

In the same way, of course, present value methods show much more precisely the greater value of cash earnings received in the early years of a project. In a sense, we can say that the payback method takes into account the time value of money very crudely. However, it does not fully measure the time–money rate of return as present value methods do. Furthermore, it totally ignores the "profits" and "cash inflows" that occur after the investment has been repaid. The residual values or cash flows are also overlooked. This particular shortcoming can be critical in a long-term investment. Thus, the payback method is an inadequate tool for the many investments that are long term and are important to a company's future growth.

As a final point, we should note that however useful it is to evaluate an investment in terms of the time period in which it will be paid back, this measurement ignores any expression of projectability or of absolute dollars. It is difficult, therefore, to meaningfully compare or rank alternative capital investments with the payback method.

In summary, we can briefly state the advantages and limitations of the payback method as follows:

ADVANTAGES
1. Easy to calculate and understand.
2. Good rough indicator for preliminary investment screening.
3. Measures cash recoverability.
4. Time expression can help evaluate investment in terms of risk.
5. Appropriately emphasizes earlier cash flows.

LIMITATIONS
1. Does not truly take into account the time value of money.
2. Does not consider benefit of earnings after investment has been repaid.
3. Has limited use as a tool to compare and rank alternative investments.

The Accounting Method

The accounting method of ROI analysis is also sometimes referred to as the book rate of return method. Either designation suggests the key feature of the method, which we noted earlier—namely that the return on an investment is measured in terms of standard accounting procedure and technique. This particular feature is not without benefit since the ultimate raison d'être for any investment, even for an employee washroom, is increased profitability. The accounting method of investment analysis helps keep this in focus. It also facilitates capital investment postmortems in order to determine whether the actual profitability of new investments is in line with the original estimates.

Although the accounting method makes use of standard accounting methods that might be somewhat confusing to a neophyte, it is also easy to calculate and understand. The method, however, suffers from the same limitation as the payback method in that it does not in any way recognize the time value of money; indeed, it gives no weight to either the amounts or the timing of cash flows. Finally, the methodology implicitly assumes that the investment and the associated savings or earnings will last for the depreciable life of the investment involved. In today's dynamic and volatile business environment, this can be a highly tenuous assumption. A machine that molds plastic *Star Wars* toys may last for 15 years; whether the faddish demand for such products will last that long is another question. The advantages and limitations of the accounting method are as follows:

ADVANTAGES
1. Emphasizes accounting profit and loss effect of investment.
2. Consistent with, and relates to, accounting data.
3. Easy to calculate.

LIMITATIONS
1. Does not recognize the time value of money.
2. Assumes investment and benefits will last for the depreciable life of the assets involved.
3. Does not give any weight to amounts or timing of cash flows.

Present Value Methods

The key feature and advantage of the present value methods of ROI analysis is that, unlike the other methods, present value methods take into account the time value of money. But there are other advantages to present value analysis, as is shown in the following excerpts from Robert Heller's wry, witty book *The Great Executive Dream:* *

> Businesses and heads of corporations don't earn profits: they earn money. Profit is an abstraction from the true, underlying movement of cash in and cash out. Any small businessman who has had trouble meeting the payroll knows the painful principle: without enough cash, you drown. Larger businessmen have learned the same lesson in the same brutal way: the mighty Penn Central in the U.S. ran out of hard currency; so did Rolls-Royce; so did a one-time British textile star, Klinger. . . . A big company's checks can rebound just as high as those of a little shopkeeper. But many top executives, even in suave and sophisticated organizations, have never mastered the truth that what counts at the end of the day is the cash in the kitty—not the abstractions in the books.

Heller's points seem well taken and they are the considerations that have led to a general preference for the use of present value methods as a tool for investment analysis. Present value methods not only concentrate exclusively on cash; they also give weight to the amounts and timing of all cash flows, including residual values, and for the entire life of the project. This aspect gives present value methods an advantage in evaluating long-term capital investment projects. Also, with the methods, projects are more easily compared or ranked, by means of the excess present value index. Finally, the methodology makes it easier to account for the real versus the depreciable life of an investment project. As was pointed out earlier, the depreciable life of a machine that makes plastic *Star Wars* toys may be 15 years; the true economic life, the period over which these toys can be sold, may be only three years.

*New York: Delacorte Press, 1972.

Ironically, the very real strengths of the present value methods also give rise to some of their limitations. Thus, the methods are extremely sophisticated, but at the same time they are much more difficult to understand. The sophistication of the present value methods can provide an aura of precision and validity to investment analysis that is unwarranted given the risk and uncertainty of basic underlying assumptions. Furthermore, if calculated manually, they are much more difficult and time-consuming than the payback or accounting methods (particularly for the DCF/IRR methods, which require "finding" the rate of return).

Present value methods center attention on money—cold, hard cash—which spells the success or failure of any business or investment, yet the resulting computations of "discounted cash flows" are not readily related to the almost as important accounting profit or loss effects.

A final limitation of all present value methods is that the methodology implicitly assumes that all cash flows from an investment can be reinvested at the rates of return that were used either to determine the desired rate of return, as in the present value method, or—as in the case of the DCF/IRR—to discount the cash flows. Let us make the point another way. The investor faces a future that begins with an outlay of funds. At the moment of decision, his or her concern is with return on that particular investment. We can assume that the return on that particular investment is equal to the rate of return indicated, but this situation occurs only if the investor is able to put the cash inflows from the investment back to work at the same rate of return.

It is important to understand the implicit reinvestment assumption in all the present value methods. We recall that in the same way the accounting method implicitly assumes that the benefits of an investment will last for the entire depreciable life of the assets involved. The present value methods' implicit reinvestment assumption should be borne in mind when you are evaluating investment projects that show extraordinarily high rates of return. The advantages and limitations of the present value methods are as follows:

ADVANTAGES
1. Measures time value of money.
2. Concentrates on cash—gives weight to both timing and amounts of cash flows.
3. Facilitates ranking and comparison of investment projects.

LIMITATIONS
1. More difficult to calculate and understand.
2. Does not readily relate to accounting—profit and loss effects.
3. Assumes cash flows can be reinvested at the same rate of return to discount the project.

The Best Method

Which is the best method? As was suggested earlier, most professionals would probably prefer, or in some cases even insist on, the present value methods. Yet all the methods have some advantages as well as limitations and then, as always, the most important element in all methods of analysis is just plain common business sense. Since the capital investment decision is such an important one, it is probably well worth the effort to use all three methods.

7

Setting the
Rate of Return

WE have reviewed the importance of ROI and have evaluated the three basic methods of calculating it. In this chapter, we will discuss how to set the rate of return or how to determine what is a good or acceptable rate of return on a new capital investment. The question is hardly academic. You may recall that the decision rule for the present value method states that a project is acceptable if, apart from nonmonetary considerations, the present value of the cash savings at the desired rate of return equals or exceeds the investment. But how do we determine a desirable rate of return? What factors should we consider? Similarly, if an investment shows an expected rate of return of 8% under the accounting method, is this acceptable? And if so, why?

Setting the rate of return is sometimes called setting the "hurdle rate," since it becomes the rate of return which all investments must "hurdle" or clear if they are to be found acceptable. There are a variety of ways to set a hurdle rate, and the first is probably the most obvious. We have referred to it often, and in Chapter 5 we called it the fundamental of all fundamentals—the compound interest rate of return of a risk-free deposit in an ordinary savings account. We also observed that from our earliest childhoods—whether we are now business professionals, executives, stockholders, or bankers—we have always ultimately compared our investment opportunities with the rate of interest that we can get from an ordinary savings account.

As of mid-1979, interest rates in the United States have soared to an all-time high. Consequently, an ordinary savings account pays a compound annual interest rate of 5.47%. Money placed in a five-year savings certificate yields 7.90%. Ninety-one-day Federal Government Treasury Bills (money loaned to the U.S. federal government for 91 days) pay an interest rate of 8.92%. Top grade corporate bonds pay 9.1%. The so-called "prime rate"—the basic interest rate banks charge their established major corporate clients stands at 11.5%.

Interest rates and yields will of course vary over time, but at any given time the cost of borrowing money and the rate paid for money in essentially risk-free investments suggest the "hurdle" rate that should be set for an investment. The reasons for this are almost self-evident: If the effortless risk-free deposit of money in a savings account will yield a return of 5.47%, why pursue a business or capital investment that returns less? Also, if funds for an investment must be borrowed at 11.5%, it hardly makes sense to use them for an investment that has a return of only 6%. Obviously, the cost of financing the investment would exceed the income that could be expected from it—hardly sound business practice.

Inflation, of course, has a significant influence on interest rates and yields, and in and of itself is an appropriate factor to consider when you are setting a hurdle rate. If a proposed investment has a return of 10%, but the value of money is declining through inflation (as it recently has been in the United States) at approximately this same rate, then any real return is illusory.

There are several other relatively simple ways to set a hurdle rate. An established company or a division can always use its historical ROI performance as a hurdle rate. (In the next chapter, we will discuss in detail the methods and significance of calculating a company's or division's historical ROI.) If the historical relationship of a company's net profits to its assets has yielded a 14% return on investment, then obviously new investments that show a projected return of 10% will decrease rather than improve the company's overall return on investment.

A company can also set a hurdle rate relationship to competitors or industry rates of return. Since ROI is such a basic and common measure of business performance, current and historical ROI data for all publicly traded corporations are readily available. A sample from the *Forbes* magazine 1977 Annual Report on American Industry* appears in Exhibit 6 as a typical example.

Although there is a variety of ready reference points for companies or investors to establish their hurdle rates, they can, of course, simply resort to an arbitrary or intuitive standard. In this case, they simply say that they won't make a capital investment unless it has a 25% return. If successful, this approach can bring about an improvement in the productivity (the return) on capital. There is always the risk, however, that the intuitive or arbitrary rate may be unrealistically high with the result that no new capital investments are undertaken. The long-term consequences of no capital investment for a business can be disastrous. If intuition is used to

*Reprinted by permission of *Forbes* magazine from the January 1, 1977, issue.

Exhibit 6. Electronics and electrical equipment: Yardsticks of management performance.

| | PROFITABILITY | | | | | | | | GROWTH | | | |
| | Return on Equity | | | | Return on Total Capital | | | | Sales | | Earnings/Share | |
Company	5-Year Average	5-Year Rank	Latest 12 Months	Debt/ Equity Ratio	Latest 12 Months	5-Year Rank	5-Year Average	Net Profit Margin	5-Year Average	5-Year Rank	5-Year Average	5-Year Rank
ELECTRICAL EQUIPMENT												
Reliance Electric	21.7%	1	25.9%	0.5	14.9%	6	13.8%	6.2%	14.4%	5	12.6%	5
W W Grainger	20.9	2	18.1	0.0	17.8	3	18.3	6.7	18.9	2	18.2	2
AMP	20.8	3	17.2	0.2	14.3	2	18.8	8.9	16.2	4	13.7	4
Square D	20.5	4	20.6	0.2	17.3	1	18.8	8.3	13.1	7	5.7	10
Emerson Electric	19.1	5	18.9	0.2	17.4	4	17.4	7.8	14.4	6	10.0	9
UV Industries	19.1	5	21.6	0.7	11.8	11	9.3	7.2	19.7	1	22.6	1
General Electric	17.9	7	17.7	0.3	14.5	5	14.5	5.1	8.0	11	10.7	6
Fischbach & Moore	17.6	8	14.0	0.5	10.2	7	13.2	1.7	18.5	3	10.6	7
Eltra	13.4	9	13.3	0.2	11.0	8	11.6	5.0	10.6	8	10.1	8
Cutler-Hammer	12.9	10	13.4	0.4	10.3	9	10.2	4.0	9.2	9	15.2	3
McGraw-Edison	10.3	11	14.5	0.2	12.9	10	9.5	5.5	7.4	12	-0.7	12
Westinghouse Elec	8.2	12	11.3	0.3	8.6	12	6.6	3.5	8.9	10	-0.3	11
Medians	**18.5**		**17.5**	**0.3**	**13.6**		**13.5**	**5.9**	**13.8**		**10.7**	
Industry Medians	**13.4**		**14.5**	**0.3**	**11.8**		**10.6**	**5.5**	**10.9**		**10.7**	
All-Industry Medians	**12.7**		**12.9**	**0.4**	**9.8**		**9.1**	**4.6**	**11.8**		**9.4**	

Note: Explanation of Yardstick calculations on page 39. P-D Profit to deficit. D-P Deficit to profit; not ranked. def Deficit.

set a hurdle rate, the investor is well reminded that many a comely maiden has died a lonely spinster for having set her standards unrealistically high.

Finally, a somewhat more complex way of establishing a hurdle rate is by the cost of capital method, to which we alluded earlier in our discussion when we pointed out that it obviously made no sense for a business to borrow money at an annual cost of 10% and then use it to make an investment whose return was 6%. As this suggests, the basic notion of the cost of capital method is that a company's minimum hurdle rate should equal the cost of its capital. At first blush this might suggest nothing more than identifying current interest costs as the appropriate investment hurdle rate. The British economist Lord Keynes expressed much the same thought when he said, "Businessmen would continue to invest as long as the return on one more dollar of investment (marginal efficiency of capital) exceeded the interest rate (marginal cost of capital)." It seems obvious that an investment yielding 25% on funds at an interest cost of 12% is a highly attractive proposition.

However, if we define the cost of capital only as current interest costs, we have implicitly assumed that borrowed funds are the only source of capital for a business. Such an assumption is unrealistic, since every business needs some permanent capital in the form of equity. As a matter of fact, the solvency of a publicly held corporation is constantly evaluated in terms of the relationship of debt (usually long-term debt, or obligations in excess of one year) to equity. A very rough rule of thumb in American business is that the owners or shareholders should have $2 invested for every $1 of debt. The credit of companies that do not meet such standards is considered to be weaker than is the credit of those that do; this in turn increases the interest rates at which they can borrow money. These few brief comments ignore the often extensive and complex financial analyses that are used to establish and monitor a company's credit worthiness; they do, however, serve to make the point that is basic to our discussion—namely, that the cost of capital must also take into consideration the cost of *equity* capital. The calculation of a company's overall cost of capital, therefore, begins with an assessment of its long-term planned capital structure, including both debt and equity.

The next step involves calculating the after-tax cost of both kinds of capital. In the case of borrowed or debt capital, the calculation is relatively straightforward: If the interest cost on long-term debt is 10% then the after-tax cost is 5.2%. (Interest expense on long-term debt at 10% is taxed at 48%, leaving an after-tax cost of 5.2%).

The calculation of the *cost of equity capital* is both more controversial and more complex. Still, most theoreticians and even practitioners agree that the basic cost is derived from the relationship between a company's *earnings per share* and the *market price* at which a share of the company's stock is publicly traded. Thus, if a company's stock has an earnings per share of $1 and it sells at a price of $10, then its cost of equity capital is 10%. The mathematical derivation of these relationships is as shown below:

$$\frac{\text{Earnings per share}}{\text{Market value per share}} = \frac{\$1.00}{\$10.00} = 10\% \text{ (cost of equity capital)}$$

The reader may readily recognize that the cost of capital is simply the conventional earnings per share multiple shown for every publicly traded common stock expressed as a percentage. The essence of the relationship, however, is that for a given company in a particular industry, a certain amount of earnings will attract a certain amount of capital. In our specific illustration, $1 of earnings attracted $10 of capital. We will return to discuss some of the nuances and anomalies of price/earnings relationships later, but for now let us examine how we use that relationship along with conventional interest costs to calculate the overall total cost of capital to a company.

As we have said, the first step is to define the expected long-term capital structure of the company, which for the purpose of illustration we shall assume conforms to the conventional ratio of $2 of equity for every $1 of debt. Thus, we have

Long-term debt	$1,000,000
Shareholders' equity	2,000,000
Total	$3,000,000

If we assume that the before-tax interest cost on the debt is 10% and that the company's stock sells at the same price/earnings ratio of 10:1 that we used in our earlier illustration, then the company's overall cost of capital would be calculated as shown below:

Type of Capital	Amount	Weighted % of Total
Debt	$1,000,000	33%
Equity	2,000,000	67%
Total	$3,000,000	100%

Step 1: Calculate the weight of debt to equity in the total long-term capital structure.

Step 2: Calculate the after-tax cost of each form of capital.

(a) Interest on long-term debt is a tax-deductible expense. Thus, 10% interest cost is reduced by taxes of 48% (or 4.8%), giving an after-tax cost of debt of 5.2%.

(b) If the company has earnings per share of common

stock at $1 and is publicly traded at $10 per share, then the cost of equity capital is 10%. The cost of this equity capital, however, is 10% on an *after-tax* basis, since the earnings per share are expressed in the form of net earnings *after tax*.

Step 3: Calculate the weighted after-tax cost of total capital for the company.

Type of Capital	Amount	Weighted % of Total	After-Tax Cost	Weighted Cost %
Debt	$1,000,000	33%	5.2%	1.7%
Equity	2,000,000	67%	10.0%	6.7%
Total	$3,000,000	100%		8.4%

The overall cost of capital after taxes, as it is calculated above, would serve as a hurdle rate below which a company should not accept an investment proposal. If it were to do so, the cost of financing the investment would be greater than the return.

We should note that the 8.4% rate may seem low; however, this is an after-tax rate. Expressed on a before-tax basis, with tax rates of 48%, it would be nearly doubled to 16.2% ($8.4\% \div 52\% = 16.15\%$). As noted earlier, we also need further discussion on the use of the price/earnings ratio as a determinant of the cost of equity. If a company has a price/earnings ratio of $20 to $1, rather than $10 to $1, does this really mean that its cost of equity capital is 5% rather than 10%? While mathematically this would seem so, in practice it would leave a company with a "cost of capital" hurdle rate so low as to make almost any investment acceptable. In a situation such as this one, a company's historical as well as its anticipated rate of earnings growth undoubtedly influences the price/earnings ratio it commands in the market. To take this factor into account, the approximate annual growth factor in excess of the industry average is added to the company's cost of equity. In our illustration, the company's basic cost of equity would thus be 5%.

$$\text{Cost of equity} = \frac{\text{earnings (\$1)}}{\text{price per share (\$20)}} = 5\%$$

If we assume that the company's earnings have grown at an annual compound rate of 18% versus an industry average of 9%, then this differential of 9% would also be added to the basic cost of equity, giving a total cost of 14%.

Exactly how precise is this determination of the cost of capital with the variation discussed here? That is highly questionable, although it undoubtedly provides a more realistic hurdle rate than would be obtained with only the basic calculation. And now, having covered the crucial process of setting the rate of return, we conclude our review of the methods and procedures for the analysis of new capital investments and turn to a discussion of ROI concepts as a measure of overall business performance.

8

ROI as a Measure of Overall Business Performance

In the preceding chapters we've discussed the importance of the return on new capital investments and methods used to measure that return. But, as we mentioned in the first chapter, ROI also provides a reliable measure of overall business performance. In fact, many consider ROI to be the only meaningful measure of a company's success.

In this chapter we will discuss how ROI is used to measure overall performance. But first a reminder: a company's performance reflects the success with which management chooses and executes new investments and the skill with which management handles old investments.

Return on overall business performance can be measured in three basic ways:

1. As return on shareholders' equity.
2. As return on total investment.
3. As return on total assets.

The ratios used to calculate the overall rate of return on business investment by each of these three methods are derived from a "balance sheet" and an "income statement," both of which are included in a company's annual statement. Simplified examples of the two schedules are shown as Exhibits 7 and 8.

Let's turn now to a detailed discussion of the three analytical methods, and examine their uses and limitations.

Return on Shareholders' Equity

The most frequently used measure of return on investment is "return on shareholders' equity," or "return on shareholders' investment." For its numerator, this ratio has the net income of the company for the period; its denomi-

Exhibit 7. Balance sheet, EZ Corporation—December 31, 1976.

	1975	1976		1975	1976
Current assets	$180	$190	Current liabilities	$ 90	$100
Net fixed assets	80	103	Bonds payable	70	70
Other assets	10	10	Shareholders' equity	110	133
Total assets	$270	$303	Total liabilities and equity	$270	$303

Exhibit 8. Income statement, EZ Corporation—period ending 1976.

Sales	$400,000
Less cost of goods sold	280,000
Gross profit	$120,000
Less selling expenses	50,000
Less administrative expenses	20,000
Operating income	$ 50,000
Less interest expense	4,200
Income before taxes	$ 45,800
Less income taxes	22,800
Net income after taxes	$ 23,000

nator is the shareholders' investment at the end of the period. So, for EZ Corporation, we have

$$\frac{\text{Net income after taxes (Exhibit 7)}}{\text{Shareholders' equity at yearend (Exhibit 6)}} = \frac{\$23,000}{\$133,000} = 17\%$$

Although the ratio for the return on shareholders' equity always consists of net income as a numerator and shareholders' investment as a denominator, the ratio can be varied by adjusting either the numerator or the denominator. In most cases the denominator changes. For example, the net income for the period can be related to shareholders' investment at the beginning of the period rather than at the end. For EZ we would then have

$$\frac{\text{Net income}}{\text{Shareholders' equity at beginning of year}} = \frac{\$23,000}{\$110,000} = 21\%$$

Another variation involves averaging the shareholders' investment at the beginning and at the end of the period. This variation gives the following return:

Shareholders' equity at beginning of year	$110,000	
Shareholders' equity at end of year	133,000	
	243,000	÷ 2 = $121,500
Average shareholders' equity during year	121,500	

$$\frac{\text{Net income}}{\text{Average shareholders' equity during year}} = \frac{23,000}{\$121,500} = 19\%$$

None of these variations is necessarily more correct than the others, although the last method given is the most frequently used. It does make sense: Shareholders have a certain investment in the corporation at the beginning and at the end of the year; the average of the two figures represents the average investment on which earnings have been generated throughout the year. But what is important in ROI—as well as in any other analysis—and the point to be emphasized here is that one must know what approach has been used in any ROI calculation and that that approach has been used consistently throughout any period included in an analysis.

In its most common form, shareholders' equity includes the shareholders' original investment plus those earnings of the corporation that have been retained for internal expansion rather than paid out to shareholders as dividends. Sometimes, the corporation incurs losses rather than earnings, however, and these losses also form part of shareholders' equity. Thus, shareholders' equity reflects any loss incurred by the corporation—that is, the shareholders' original investment is reduced by the corporation's accumulated losses.

In order to provide a meaningful calculation of the return on the shareholders' equity when a company experiences losses, the net income should be related to the shareholders' original investment rather than to shareholders' equity. Exhibit 9 shows the different results obtained when net income is related to shareholders' equity and when it is related to shareholders' original investment:

Exhibit 9.

Net Income Related to Shareholders' Equity

Shareholders' original investment	$1,000,000
Retained earnings (losses)	(200,000)
Shareholders' equity	800,000
Net income for period	80,000

$$\frac{\text{Net income for period}}{\text{Shareholders' equity}} = \frac{80,000}{800,000} = 10\%$$

Return on shareholders' equity = 10%

Net Income Related to Shareholders' Original Investment

Net income for period	$ 80,000
Shareholders' original investment	1,000,000

Return on shareholders' original investment = 8%

As its name suggests, the return on shareholders' equity quantifies the return on their investment that the shareholders receive over a specified period of time. But the ratio is also a significant measure of how well the shareholders (through their elected board of directors) have managed the overall business and of how intelligently and how profitably management has used its custodianship.

For these reasons, return on shareholders' equity (as well as other return calculations that we will discuss) forms a key part of any objective evaluation of the current and prospective profitability and financial position of any business. Such evaluations are prepared by the services such as Standard & Poor's and Moody's, and by leading financial publications such as *Fortune* and *Forbes*.

We should note that the return to the shareholder indicated by the ratio does not necessarily mean that the shareholder will receive that amount in cash. Corporate shareholders receive the cash return from their investment in the form of dividends. Although it is conceivable that a corporation might distribute 100% of each year's annual earnings as dividends, this is highly unlikely; some portion is usually retained in the business to finance further growth. We should also note that the investment included in the ratio is that of an original shareholder—the shareholder who subscribed to the stock of the corporation when it was originally issued. If the company has enjoyed some success, then in all likelihood new shareholders will have paid a premium for their stock investments. Thus, the return they enjoy will be the net income they receive in relation to the price they paid for the stock, not the original subscription price.

Finally it would be in order to reemphasize the significance of return ratios in light of the accelerated and sometimes double-digit inflation experienced by most of the industrialized nations of the world. If a company fails to generate an ROI that is at least equal to the annual rate of inflation in the economy in which it has primary operations, the company is being decapitalized. Such a situation may seem unlikely, but far from it: It is already taking place. In 1975 more than 200 of the top 500 corporations in the United States had a return on shareholders' investment of less than 9% at a time when the U.S. dollar lost its purchasing power at an annual rate of 9% through inflation. And because of the high rates of inflation anticipated in the future, the economic environment will certainly continue to put a premium on skillful management of capital in the years ahead.

Return on Total Investment

The second method for determining return on investment is to calculate return on total capital. In this ratio the numera-tor is once again the net income of the corporation for the ap-

Exhibit 10. Return on total capital employed.

Net income after tax		$ 23,000
Add back interest on long-term debt		
Interest before tax	4,200	
Less tax deduction on interest expense at 48%	2,100	
Interest expense after tax		2,100
Net income after tax adjusted for interest		$ 25,100
Total Capital		
Long-term debt		$ 70,000
Shareholders' equity		133,000
		$203,000

$$\frac{\text{Net income} + \text{interest after tax}}{\text{Total capital}} = \frac{\$ 25,100}{\$203,000} = 12.4\%$$

propriate period. The denominator, however, includes long-term permanent capital—funds borrowed for more than one year—in addition to shareholders' equity.

As shown in Exhibit 10, the first stage of calculating the return on total investment involves adjusting net income for the effect of the interest paid on the long-term capital. To do this we simply add the interest on long-term debt to the net income after tax. We know from EZ's income statement (Exhibit 8) that the annual interest cost on long-term debt was $4,200. But here we have a problem: The interest cost of $4,200 was determined before income taxes, and must be adjusted if it is to be added to income items that are on an after-tax basis. This can be done easily by multiplying the interest cost by the tax factor (48% for corporations) and subtracting that amount from the interest cost. As we see from Exhibit 10, the net income after tax plus interest adjusted for taxes amounts to $25,100.

As we mentioned before, the denominator consists of shareholders' equity plus the long-term debt of the corporation. For EZ Corporation, the denominator is $203,000 ($70,000 of long-term debt plus $133,000 of shareholders' equity). EZ Corporation's return on total investment is 12.4%.

The return on total capital is valuable because it indicates the return earned on *all long-term sources* of funds employed in the business, not only shareholders' investments. This ratio almost always accompanies the more basic and conventional return on shareholders' investment. If we look at Exhibit 11, we can better appreciate why.

Exhibit 11 shows the financial information presented for EZ Corporation in Exhibits 7 and 8 with comparable data for a competitor. The competitor appears to be considerably more successful: it has a higher return on shareholders' investment (21% compared to 17% for EZ). But let's look at Exhibit 12. Here we see that both companies enjoy exactly the same return on total capital. The difference between the two companies is not that one earns a higher return on its investments than the other, but that their permanent capital is

Exhibit 11. Comparative ROIs: EZ Corporation vs. competitor.

	EZ Corporation	Competitor
Long-term debt	$ 70,000	$100,000
Shareholders' equity	133,000	103,000
Total capital	$203,000	$203,000
Net income	$ 23,000	$ 22,100
Annual interest expense	4,200	6,000
Annual interest expense adjusted for taxes at 50%	2,100	3,000

Calculation of Return on Shareholders' Investment		
Reported net income	$ 23,000 / $133,000	$ 22,100 / $103,000
Percent return on shareholders' equity	17%	21%

Exhibit 12. Comparative ROIs: EZ Corporation vs. competitor.

	EZ Corporation	Competitor
Reported net income	$ 23,000	$ 22,100
Add back annual interest expense adjusted for taxes	2,100	3,000
Totals	$ 25,100	$ 25,100

Calculation of Return on Total Capital

$$\frac{\text{Reported net income adjusted for interest expense}}{\text{Total capital}} =$$

	EZ Corporation	Competitor
Reported net income adjusted for interest expense	$25,100	$25,100
Total capital	$203,000	$203,000
Percent return on total capital	12%	12%

structured differently. Specifically, the competitor has a higher proportion of long-term debt as part of its total capital than does the EZ Corporation.

In the jargon of the financial community, the competitor is said to be more "leveraged," which may or may not be to its advantage. Nevertheless, the analysis of the return on total capital isolates the contribution of a major proportion of *long-term debt to* the appearance of higher profitability.

It should be noted that the return on total investment can be varied in the same ways as can the return on shareholders' equity: It can be based on total capital at both the beginning and end of the period and on the average total capital for the year.

Note also that in the illustrations of the return calculations taken from *Forbes* (Exhibit 6), the return on total capital almost always accompanies the return on shareholders' investment calculation. You can also see that return on total capital almost always indicates a *lower* rate of return, because the addition of long-term debt to the investment denominator is much larger than the addition of the interest expense after tax to the income numerator.

Return on Total Assets

As its name suggests, the return on total assets calculation relates net income to all assets of the company. Thus, all items on the left-hand side of the company's balance sheet are included in the denominator.

There are those who insist that return on total assets is the best measure of return because the other return calculations do not take short-term financing into account. They claim that short-term financing strongly influences the return calculation. By calculating return on total assets, no such distortion is possible because debt is not considered at all. Let's take another look at the EZ Corporation. Once again we must adjust net income to reflect after-tax interest expense. So once again the numerator consists of net income plus interest expense adjusted for taxes, a total of $25,100. The denominator is the total assets of the EZ Corporation—$303,000. The return on total assets is 8.3%, as shown in Exhibit 13.

Exhibit 13. Return on Total Assets

Net income after taxes	$23,000
Plus interest expense after income taxes	2,100
Net income adjusted for interest after taxes	$25,100

$$\frac{\text{Adjusted net income}}{\text{Total assets}} = \frac{\$25,100}{\$303,000} = 8.3\% \text{ return on total assets}$$

You will note that return on total assets is even lower than the return on total investment because once again the investment denominator has increased at a much greater rate than has the profit numerator.

Some General Considerations

Although we have confined our discussion of return on investment to its function as a measure of overall business performance, we should note that ROI is used extensively within corporate organizations as a managerial tool and as a yardstick of managerial performance. With the growth in size and complexity of modern corporations, responsibility for the everyday operations and for profitability is more and more being delegated to lower levels of the organization. Middle managers are responsible for the profits of those areas for which they have custodianship. These areas are called "profit centers". The establishment of profit centers has led to "return on investment centers" (see Chapter 9). So, middle managers who head up ROI centers are given responsibility not only for profits but also for management of those assets used to generate the profits. ROI centers now form a common part of large organizations in the United States and other industrialized nations.

Later on we will go into a more detailed discussion of the internal applications of ROI analytical techniques. But for now we must recognize that ROI is often used as a technique for the evaluation not only of the value of business but also of managerial performance. These evaluations can be made under any one of the ROI analytical techniques discussed in the preceding pages. Interestingly enough, they may come up with results that appear to contradict the facts. For example, the return on a particular ROI center may be nominal—say, 4% to 6% a year. In the face of more attractive investment alternatives and even the going cost of short-term money at 7% a year, top management might well conclude that it should disinvest that center. But if the return on that center in earlier periods had been lower, or even nonexistent, that would be an indication that the manager responsible for that center has

size, and complexity of the modern business organization have led to decentralization. Quite simply, decentralization means that the responsibility and authority for the profitable operation of commercial activities is delegated to small, manageable components of the enterprise. Organizational and accounting controls are developed to evaluate how effectively the manager of each of these components carries out his responsibilities.

These components, called "responsibility centers," take several forms, one of the most basic of which is the "revenue center." A segment of the organization is given responsibility for generating revenues to meet a specified target. The sales department of almost any organization is a good example of a revenue center. There, the revenue targets are the salesperson's dreaded annual sales "commitments".

The second kind of responsibility center, used at least as much, as the revenue center, if not more so, is the "cost center." A segment of the organization is given responsibility for controlling costs of operations over which it has authority. Almost all private and public organizations now use cost centers.

Although revenue and cost centers are useful in decentralization, they have obvious limitations. A revenue center isolates the responsibility for the generation of revenues, but does not indicate the costs incurred to obtain the revenues. On the other hand, a cost center facilitates the control of costs, but does not measure the revenues generated as a result of the costs incurred. Some typical examples of cost centers might be a controller's office or a legal department.

The critical failure of the revenue and cost centers to match revenues against costs led to the development of the "profit center." Profit-center management is delegated the responsibility both for generating revenues and for controlling costs associated with those revenues.

Most large corporations and organizations today have profit centers for obvious reasons: The profit center focuses on a basic business objective—profitability. But despite the advantages of the profit center concept, it has one major defect: it does not take into account the fact that profits are relative. Let's look at two profit centers. Profit Center A earns $200,000 a year, whereas Profit Center B earns $400,000 a year:

	Profit Center A	Profit Center B
Net income	$ 200,000	$ 400,000
Investment	$1,000,000	$2,000,000
Return on investment	20%	20%

Profit center B would appear to be more profitable by far. But we know that any assessment based only on this information is premature and very possibly erroneous, since we have ignored a critical consideration—what funds have been invested to generate these profits.

Using these examples, we can see that if the investment is $1,000,000 in Profit Center A and $2,000,000 in Profit Center B, then the two centers are equally successful because they are both earning a 20% return on their investment.

The necessity of clarifying the relationship between profit and the investment used in generating that profit has led to the application of ROI to the responsibility concept. And so we have the final and most sophisticated form of the responsibility center—the ROI control center.

Managers of ROI control centers are delegated responsibility not only for the profitability of an operation but also for the most efficient use of the assets they control and that are used to generate that profit. The ROI center approach gives managers the incentive to deploy their capital intelligently.

We have already learned how important having an objective is to the overall performance of the corporation.

The Residual Income Concept

Practically everybody agrees on the importance of adequate return on investment, but not everybody agrees that the ROI-center approach is the best method for measuring ROI. As we have seen, return on investment is derived from the relationship between profits and investment, and it's precisely this aspect that critics find objectionable. They argue that ROI is an index, and that ROI tempts management merely to maximize the index rather than to maximize the *absolute* profits in relation to the capital employed.

One can more readily appreciate this point in the context of a personal investment situation. Would you, ask the critics, rather have a $10,000 investment yielding a 20% return or a $200,000 investment yielding a 12% return? The ready answer, for most of us, is that we would choose the greater investment income over the dramatically higher rate of return. But, say the critics, the conventional application of the ROI formula would encourage you to choose the investment with the higher return even though the actual amount of income would be less.

Out of concerns and criticisms such as these has come an adaptation of the ROI center approach called "the residual income" concept. Let's explore this concept by first looking at a comparison of two ROI centers based on the application of the standard ROI concepts.

In the conventional ROI calculation shown on p. 88, ROI Center A would appear to be more successful than ROI Center B. Critics of ROI, however, would argue that Center

	Business A	Business B
Investment base	$1,000	$5,000
Net income	200	750
ROI	20%	15%

A merely has a higher index. The real question, they would say, is whether it is better to earn a high rate of return on a small amount of capital or a modest rate of return on a larger amount of capital. To evaluate the performance of the two centers from this perspective, each center should be charged with its "cost of capital." This cost is deducted from the stated profit of the center to arrive at the "residual income"—the income that remains after the cost of capital has been deducted. If we assume, for example, that the cost of capital applicable to the investments in both ROI Centers A and B is 12%, their comparative performance would appear as follows:

Net income	$200	$750
Less cost of capital	120	600
Residual income	$ 80	$150

Under the residual income concept, ROI Center B makes a greater absolute contribution to profits, even though it has the lower ROI ratio. Proponents of the residual income concept argue that this is a more relevant measure of performance than is the rate of return and that the residual income concept provides a tool for the internal evaluation of managerial performance because:

1. It allows management to set absolute goals or standards for performance rather than merely to define an index of performance.

2. Different costs of capital can be applied to different segments of the business. The cost of capital applied to each

segment reflects the degree of risk and the age of assets employed, thereby providing a more accurate assessment of the cost of capital than can be achieved by applying an overall rate.

3. When it is appropriate to do so, the same cost of capital can be applied to all assets, thereby allowing a direct comparison between profit performance of different ROI centers.

All of these advantages suggest that the residual income concept is preferable to the conventional ROI approach to managerial control and evaluation.

But the residual income concept is not without problems. Suppose, for example, that the cost of capital used in our previous illustrations is now 18% instead of 12%. The residual income of each operation would then be:

Net income	$200	$750
Less cost of capital	180	900
Residual income	$ 20	$(150)

As we can see, the residual income concept cannot point to the more successful ROI centers. The choice of the rate of return earned on the capital employed is obviously of overriding importance. Indeed, an objective evaluation of "residual income performance" can only be as meaningful as the choice of the rate of return applied to the capital employed. On the other hand, it can be argued that even though residual income profitability at different costs of capital may vary, the cost of capital (and hence, of true profitability) is totally obscured under the standard ROI approach. Thus, control systems based on the ROI concept can be used as an aid to, but never as a substitute for, good common-sense judgment. Nevertheless, ROI systems have—and will continue to have—significant influence on organization design and control.

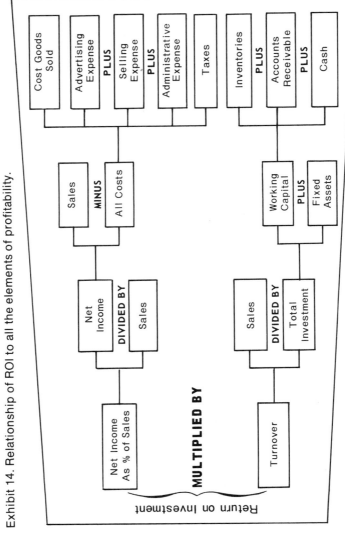

Exhibit 14. Relationship of ROI to all the elements of profitability.

Components of ROI

Although ROI is expressed as a single percentage, we can see from Exhibit 14 that it encompasses all the elements that go together to make up the profitability of a business organization. The comprehensiveness of the ROI calculation is a significant factor.

We can further note that return on investment calculation is the result of the interplay between two important aspects of the business: the rate of profit earned on sales (net profit ÷ sales), and the rate at which the assets employed in the business are "turned over" (sales ÷ investment). Generally speaking, profitability depends on sound control of costs and on adequate pricing as well as successful selling. Turnover depends on the effective use of assets—both working capital and fixed investments—that are used to generate sales.

Businesses use different combinations of profit and turnover ratios to generate an adequate return on their investments (see Exhibit 15). Business A and Business B enjoy exactly the same return but achieve it in dramatically different ways.

Exhibit 15. ROI components.

	Company A Fast Pennies	Company B Slow Nickels
Sales	$5,000,000	$5,000,000
Net income	50,000	250,000
Investment	$500,000	$2,500,000
Net income as % sales	1%	5%
Investment turnover	10	2
ROI	1% × 10 = 10%	2% × 5 = 10%

The turnover-to-profitability relationship provides a useful concept for incisive ROI analysis evaluation of ROI performance.

Other ROI Applications

Although ROI analysis has found its greatest use in the measurement of overall corporate and ROI control center performance, other applications of this important management tool are almost unlimited. Take, for example, the not uncommon business proposal for a sales-force expansion into two new districts. Assume that the estimated increases in sales and in operating profits for such an expansion are as shown in Exhibit 16. On the basis of these figures, it would appear that the district market expansion into Atlanta would produce the same results as expansion into Cleveland.

But you might also note that the all-important consideration—what investment must be made to support these expansions—has been ignored. Many make the mistake of assuming that because this is only a marketing expansion, no investment is involved. Nothing could be further from the truth. Investments are often thought of only in terms of additions to property, plant, and equipment, but in fact the "working capital" used to support a sales effort is a permanent investment. Working capital includes the accounts receivable (the credit that must nearly always be given to customers) and the product inventories that must be maintained to service purchase requests promptly.

Exhibit 16. ROI analysis of district market expansion.

	Atlanta	Cleveland
Expected increase in:		
Sales	$100,000	$100,000
Cost of goods sold	55,000	55,000
Gross margin	45,000	45,000
Marketing costs	15,000	15,000
Operating profit	$30,000	$30,000

Exhibit 17. More detailed ROI analysis of district market expansion.

	Atlanta	Cleveland
Expected increase in:		
Sales	$100,000	$100,000
Cost of goods sold	55,000	55,000
Gross margin	$ 45,000	$ 45,000
Marketing costs	15,000	15,000
Operating profit	$ 30,000	$ 30,000
· Accounts receivable	17,000	25,000
Inventories	33,000	10,000
Total investment	$ 50,000	$ 35,000
Profit on sales	30%	30%
Investment turnover	2.0 times	2.9 times
Return on assets managed (ROAM)	60%	86%

Keep in mind that the investment in property, plant, and equipment is recovered not only through the earnings of the facility, but also through the annual depreciation charges, which are not actual cash charges. In contrast, the investments that must be made to maintain the receivables and inventories are permanent investments and can be reduced only by means of absolute decreases in the amounts of accounts receivable inventory levels outstanding at any one time. So any marketing effort requires an investment of working capital, as is shown in Exhibit 17.

We can see that once the working capital investment required to support the market expansions is identified (assuming of course, that the estimates are reasonable), Cleveland is found to be a more attractive location than Atlanta. By using the turnover-to-profitability approach to ROI analysis, we can see that the higher return in Cleveland is the result of more frequent turnover of assets than is anticipated for Atlanta.

The ROI approach can be used not only to analyze initial investment but also to monitor performance. So the approach can be used to evaluate the Cleveland district manager's performance—how well he or she meets sales objectives and controls marketing costs, and how well he or she manages the accounts receivable and inventories used to generate these sales. Sales managers cannot simply emphasize "volume"; they must operate in an overall business context and attempt to optimize the return on investment.

The application of the return on investment concept to the sales/marketing function, which was illustrated above and in Exhibit 17, is often referred to as *ROAM*—return on assets managed—and is gaining widespread use.

Analysis of ROI by Product

An additional and even more probing application of ROI analysis is the analysis of ROI by individual product. In the last decade, both theoreticians and practitioners of cost accounting have placed increased emphasis on the identification of "product profitability." A detailed discussion of the methods and the complexities of this application of ROI are beyond our purpose here. But the point is that it can be done. Exhibit 18 shows what a typical product profit statement might look like under the "contribution concept" or "product profitability."

As important as profitability by product may be, even more meaningful is the return on investment by product. Even though it is difficult to identify ROI by product, it is by no means impossible. For example, we pointed out earlier that any product requires a working capital investment in both receivables and inventories. In product ROI analysis,

Exhibit 18. Analysis of ROI by products, EZ Corporation.

	Product X	Product Y	Product Z	Total
Sales	$230,000	$125,000	$42,000	$397,000
Less variable costs				
Production	125,000	70,000	20,000	215,000
Marketing— commissions	15,000	6,000	2,000	23,000
Marketing— transportation	7,000	2,400	500	9,900
Total variable costs	$147,000	$78,400	$22,500	$247,900
Contribution after variable costs	83,000	46,600	19,500	149,100
Less direct fixed costs				
Production	15,000	8,000	3,000	26,000
Marketing	10,000	8,000	3,000	21,000
Total direct fixed costs	25,000	16,000	6,000	47,000
Product contribution	$ 58,000	$ 30,600	$13,500	$102,100
Less indirect fixed expenses				
Manufacturing				20,000
Selling				20,000
Administrative				10,000
Total indirect fixed expenses				50,000
Operating profit				$ 52,100

the level of receivables and of inventories associated with each product needs to be identified.

The next step is to identify the investment in plant and manufacturing facilities associated with the product. This analysis may present some difficulties. If a single product is manufactured in a single location and all the plant and equipment is used in manufacturing that product, then of course there will be no problem. Unfortunately, more often a variety of products is manufactured in the same factory and some-

Exhibit 19. More detailed ROI analysis by product, EZ Corporation.

	Product X	Product Y	Product Z	Total
Sales	$230,000	$125,000	$42,000	$397,000
Less variable costs				
Production	125,000	70,000	20,000	215,000
Marketing— commissions	15,000	6,000	2,000	23,000
Marketing— transportation	7,000	2,400	500	9,900
Total variable costs	147,000	78,400	22,500	247,900
Contribution after variable costs	83,000	46,600	19,500	149,100
Less direct fixed costs				
Production	15,000	8,000	3,000	26,000
Marketing	10,000	8,000	3,000	21,000
Total direct fixed costs	25,000	16,000	6,000	47,000
Product contribution	$ 58,000	$ 30,600	$13,500	$102,100
Less indirect fixed expenses				
Manufacturing				20,000
Selling				20,000
Administrative				10,000
Total indirect fixed expenses				50,000
Operating profit				$ 52,100
Investment by Product				
Receivables	46,000	25,000	5,000	76,000
Inventories	40,000	20,000	10,000	70,000
Direct production investment	150,000	40,000	60,000	250,000
Indirect production investment	40,000	30,000	30,000	100,000
Total investment	276,000	115,000	105,000	496,000
% Return product contribution to investment	21.0	26.6	12.9	20.5
% Return total group operating profit to investment	—	—	—	10.5

times even on the same equipment. When this is the case, the analyst is faced with the problem of allocating portions of the investment to each individual product.

Again, it is not within the scope of this book to present a detailed discussion of such an effort; it suffices to say that such an allocation *is* possible. The accuracy of the allocation can always be disputed, but isn't it better to attempt an analysis than to ignore it totally? Exhibit 19 shows what an ROI analysis of the products used in our preceding example might look like.

From this exhibit, it is evident that the product that first appears most desirable may not be when we have identified the associated investments. For example, whereas Product X appeared to have the highest profitability, Product Y is in fact the most successful on an ROI basis.

Much has been written about the problems and challenges that face the manager of private business in the future. There is universal agreement that the increasing scarcity of capital is one of the most significant of these challenges. Basic ROI Analysis—along with its many applications and variations—will continue to be an important tool in the analysis and evaluation of business's efforts to use this increasingly scarce resource to its fullest.

10

ROI in the
World of Inflation

THERE would seem to be little argument that inflation has become a pervasive and pernicious economic fact of life. Opinion polls show that in almost every country of the world people now see inflation as the biggest threat to their personal well-being. Everyone seems to want to reduce inflation, but not when it means a cutback in government or public services that benefit them—even though those services are perennially financed by inflationary deficit spending. Reductions in real personal income generate even less enthusiasm as a remedy. The result, unfortunately, is that inflation seems to be the kind of problem that Mark Twain had in mind when he commented, "Everyone complains about the weather, but no one seems to do much about it."

Regrettably, the hard facts of the matter sustain this perspective. For example, the International Monetary Fund recently reported that "by the end of 1977" the rate of inflation was close to 7% in industrialized countries compared with about 5% in 1969 and less than 2% in 1960. In the United States alone, the change in the Consumer Price Index is now running at the "explosive" annual rate of 13%—over double the rate of 5.9% that was a matter of concern ten years ago. Although everybody hopes for victory in the war on inflation, there seems to be little likelihood that inflation will decrease dramatically in the near future.

Therefore, to be realistic, professionals and managers at all levels must accept the adverse effects of inflation as a challenge to the sound, profitable management of their businesses. In this chapter, we will discuss how ROI concepts can be useful in this important management problem. First, however, we need to continue with a more general discussion of the broad impact of inflation on the economy of the United States and of other industrialized countries.

Undoubtedly, the most significant and personal effect of inflation is its erosion of real purchasing power. Consumers in the United States are painfully aware that a 1978 dollar buys about half as many goods and services as a 1968 dollar did. Many other countries have seen an even faster erosion of their currencies. Inflation also reduces real income in another way. Income in the United States and many other countries is taxed at progressive rates. Under such a system, as people move into higher tax brackets, the government takes more and more of their already inflated dollars, thereby squeezing their "real income" even further.

As painful as a reduction in real income may be at a personal level, the final effect is of macroeconomic significance. As real income is squeezed, personal earnings decline because more and more income must be used to maintain a "real wage." Also, people find less incentive to save when they see that the purchasing power of their savings will be eroded by inflation.

Inflation and Capital Formation

What people earn is either spent for consumption or saved for the future. Inflation deters saving, yet the formation of private capital has no other source than saving. Private saving builds a nation's stock of private capital which comprises the financial resources that must be used not only to maintain and modernize its private industrial sector but also to fund its public goals. Capital formation operates on the same basic principles as private savings, although on a larger scale. (In passing, we should also note that governmental tax policies— to the extent that they tax savings rather than consumption— can also play an important role in the rate of capital formation.)

There is now a growing concern that the United States faces a significant capital shortage in the immediate future. Reginald Jones, Chief Executive of General Electric Company, has estimated that the cumulative capital needs of the United States between 1975 and 1985 would be in the area of $3 trillion to $5 trillion. A 1977 study published by the Financial Executives Institute states that "the accumulated savings shortfall (for the United States) assuming no change in the price level will be $816 billion for the decade. At a 3% a year inflation rate, the shortfall would increase to $983 billion, and at a 5% rate it would increase to $1.113 trillion." [1]

Inflation not only slows capital formation; it also increases capital requirements, which compounds the problem. As inflation increases, the amount of dollars required to fund inventories and receivables rises, as does the cost of adding new plant capacity. Robert H. Smith, Senior Vice-President of Corporate Development for ITT, notes that companies now need about 81¢ in assets to make $1.00 in sales. Twenty

[1] "The Effects of Tax Policy on Capital Formation," Financial Executives Research Foundation, 1977.

years ago, he says, the typical company needed just 61¢.[2]

Inflation increases not only the amount of capital required, but also its cost: It is no coincidence that both inflation and interest rates are currently at an all-time high in this country. The cost of debt must take into account the cost of real money as a commodity plus some recognition of the real purchasing power of repaying the principal. (Risk and administrative costs would also be taken into account.) With real purchasing power devaluing at annual double-digit rates, a return to the era of 5%–6% interest rates on long-term debt seems remote.

Finally, inflation takes its toll in the distortion of "reported" corporate profits. A recent cover story in *Business Week* stated the problem succinctly:

> On paper, U.S. business earned a record $202 billion before taxes last year and $118 billion after—in each case 16% more than it earned in 1977 and 68% more than it earned in 1975, when the current economic expansion was just getting under way. . . . Unfortunately . . . only on paper did last year produce a boom in corporate profits. Fully one-third of the earnings that companies reported for 1978 were an illusion—gains created by inflation and out-of-date accounting methods.[2]

But not only is the amount of reported profits illusory; corporations are also showing lower returns on their assets and a greater gap "between reported and adjusted profits" than a decade ago.

In summary, as a result of inflation it seems likely that capital will become an increasingly scarce resource. Its accumulation will slow, yet its need and cost will increase. With these facts in mind, Dr. Neil H. Jacoby, Professor of Business Economics and Policy at UCLA, commented as follows:

[2] "The Profit Illusion," *Business Week,* March 19, 1979.

The economic environment will put a premium on skillful management of capital in the years ahead. In the future, skillful capital budgeting could spell the difference between survival and oblivion.[3]

Profits vs. Return on Invested Capital

Although the distorting effect of inflation on reported corporate earnings does not go entirely unnoticed, rampant inflation is a relatively new phenomenon, and tradition dies slowly. As a result, profits—no matter how illusory they may be under today's conditions—continue to be the primary bench mark for measuring corporate and business performance. Profits *are* important, but even without the current distorting effects of inflation, they are not the whole answer. The earnings of a business may be large or small, but when all is said and done, the income of the enterprise really tells us very little unless we know how much investment was required to generate it.

We can illustrate this point if we take a simple example of a company whose initial capital is represented by 1,000 shares of common stock issued at $10 per share. (And here we are expressing profits in terms of earnings per share— EPS—which is the total corporate net income divided by the number of common shares outstanding.) Assume that the first year's earnings are $1,000 and increase thereafter at an annual rate of approximately 5%. No dividends are paid, since 100% of each year's earnings are "ploughed back" (retained) in the business. At the end of four years, the company would have an earnings/EPS profile as shown in Table 12, which indicates an increase in earnings of 15% from the first

[3] *Nation's Business,* August 1976.

Table 12.

Year	Annual Net Earnings	Shares Outstanding	Earnings Per Share (EPS)
1	$1,000	1,000	$1.00
2	1,050	1,000	1.05
3	1,100	1,000	1.10
4	1,150	1,000	1.15

through the fourth years. The company's return on invested capital is shown in Table 13.

From this example, we can see that even at a meager 5% a year growth in earnings, an exclusive focus on earnings or on EPS as a measurement gives the impression of progress. From the more realistic perspective of return on invested capital, however, we see a 13% drop.

In the growing competition for capital, the need for the better utilization of existing and prospective capital resources seems obvious. Recently, the chairman of a highly capital-intensive company expressed much the same thought when he said: "Everyone recognizes that the name of the game is changing, and that the rules of the game are changing. But

Table 13. Return on invested capital (original investment: 1,000 shares at $10 per share = $10,000).

Year	Annual Net Earnings	Invested Capital	Return on Invested Capital (percent)
0	—	—	—
1	$1,000	$10,000	10.0
2	1,050	11,000	9.5
3	1,100	12,050	9.1
4	1,150	13,150	8.7

the fact that the scoring of the game must change has not dawned on many people yet.''

The ROI concepts we have discussed in this book can serve as important management tools to more accurately ''score'' the success of new as well as existing business endeavors in a changing, highly inflationary world.

Appendix A
Compound Interest Tables

Appendix B
Present Value Tables

Appendix A. Compound interest tables.

Year	1%	2%	3%	4%	5%	6%	7%	8%	9%	10%
1	1.010	1.020	1.030	1.040	1.050	1.060	1.070	1.080	1.090	1.100
2	1.020	1.040	1.061	1.082	1.102	1.124	1.145	1.166	1.188	1.210
3	1.030	1.061	1.093	1.125	1.156	1.191	1.225	1.260	1.295	1.331
4	1.041	1.082	1.126	1.170	1.216	1.262	1.311	1.360	1.412	1.464
5	1.051	1.104	1.159	1.217	1.276	1.338	1.403	1.469	1.539	1.611
6	1.062	1.120	1.194	1.265	1.340	1.419	1.501	1.587	1.677	1.772
7	1.072	1.149	1.230	1.316	1.477	1.504	1.606	1.714	1.828	1.949
8	1.083	1.172	1.267	1.369	1.477	1.594	1.718	1.851	1.993	2.144
9	1.094	1.195	1.305	1.423	1.551	1.689	1.838	1.999	2.172	2.358
10	1.105	1.219	1.344	1.480	1.629	1.791	1.967	2.159	2.367	2.594
11	1.116	1.243	1.384	1.539	1.710	1.898	2.105	2.332	2.580	2.853
12	1.127	1.268	1.426	1.601	1.796	2.012	2.252	2.518	2.813	3.138
13	1.138	1.294	1.469	1.665	1.886	2.133	2.410	2.720	3.066	3.452
14	1.149	1.319	1.513	1.732	1.980	2.261	2.579	2.937	3.342	3.797
15	1.161	1.346	1.558	1.801	2.079	2.397	2.759	3.172	3.642	4.177
16	1.173	1.373	1.605	1.873	2.183	2.540	2.952	3.426	3.970	4.595
17	1.184	1.400	1.653	1.948	2.292	2.693	3.159	3.700	4.328	5.054
18	1.196	1.428	1.702	2.026	2.407	2.854	3.380	3.996	4.717	5.560
19	1.208	1.457	1.754	2.107	2.527	3.026	3.617	4.316	5.142	6.116
20	1.220	1.486	1.806	2.191	2.653	3.207	3.870	4.661	5.604	6.728
25	1.282	1.641	2.094	2.666	3.386	4.292	5.427	6.848	8.632	10.835
30	1.348	1.811	2.427	3.243	4.322	5.743	7.612	10.063	13.268	17.449

Year	12%	14%	16%	18%	20%	24%	28%	32%	40%	50%
1	1.120	1.140	1.160	1.180	1.200	1.240	1.280	1.320	1.400	1.500
2	1.254	1.300	1.346	1.392	1.440	1.538	1.638	1.742	1.960	2.250
3	1.405	1.482	1.561	1.643	1.728	1.907	2.067	2.300	2.744	3.375
4	1.574	1.689	1.811	1.939	2.074	2.364	2.684	3.036	3.842	5.062
5	1.762	1.925	2.100	2.288	2.488	2.932	3.436	4.007	5.378	7.594
6	1.974	2.195	2.436	2.700	2.986	3.635	4.398	5.290	7.530	11.391
7	2.211	2.502	2.826	3.185	3.583	4.508	5.629	6.983	10.541	17.086
8	2.476	2.853	3.278	3.759	4.300	5.590	7.206	9.217	14.758	25.629
9	2.773	3.252	3.803	4.435	5.160	6.931	9.223	12.166	20.661	38.443
10	3.106	3.707	4.411	5.234	6.192	8.594	11.806	16.060	28.925	57.665
11	3.479	4.226	5.117	6.176	7.430	10.657	15.112	21.199	40.496	86.498
12	3.896	4.818	5.936	7.288	8.916	13.215	19.343	27.983	56.694	129.746
13	4.363	5.492	6.886	8.599	10.699	16.386	24.759	36.937	79.372	194.619
14	4.887	6.261	7.988	10.147	12.839	20.319	31.691	48.757	111.120	291.929
15	5.474	7.138	9.266	11.074	15.407	25.196	40.565	64.350	155.568	437.894
16	6.130	8.137	10.748	14.129	18.488	31.243	51.923	84.954	217.795	656.840
17	6.866	9.276	12.468	16.672	22.186	38.741	66.461	112.140	304.914	985.260
18	7.690	10.575	14.463	19.673	26.623	48.039	85.071	148.020	426.879	1477.900
19	8.613	12.056	16.777	23.214	31.948	59.568	108.890	195.390	597.630	2216.800
20	9.646	13.743	19.461	27.393	38.338	73.864	139.380	257.920	836.683	3325.300
25	17.000	26.462	40.874	62.669	95.396	216.542	478.900	1033.600	4499.880	25251.000
30	29.960	50.950	85.850	143.371	237.376	634.820	1645.500	4142.100	24201.432	191750.000

Appendix B. Present value tables.

Year	1%	2%	3%	4%	5%	6%	7%	8%	9%	10%
1	0.9901	0.9804	0.9709	0.9615	0.9524	0.9434	0.9346	0.9259	0.9174	0.9091
2	0.9803	0.9612	0.9426	0.9246	0.9070	0.8900	0.8734	0.8573	0.8417	0.8264
3	0.9706	0.9423	0.9151	0.8890	0.8638	0.8396	0.8163	0.7938	0.7722	0.7513
4	0.9610	0.9238	0.8885	0.8548	0.8227	0.7921	0.7629	0.7350	0.7084	0.6830
5	0.9515	0.9057	0.8626	0.8219	0.7835	0.7473	0.7130	0.6806	0.6499	0.6209
6	0.9420	0.8880	0.8375	0.7903	0.7462	0.7050	0.6663	0.6302	0.5963	0.5645
7	0.9327	0.8706	0.8131	0.7599	0.7107	0.6651	0.6227	0.5835	0.5470	0.5132
8	0.9235	0.8535	0.7894	0.7307	0.6768	0.6274	0.5820	0.5403	0.5019	0.4665
9	0.9143	0.8368	0.7664	0.7026	0.6446	0.5919	0.5439	0.5002	0.4604	0.4241
10	0.9053	0.8203	0.7441	0.6756	0.6139	0.5584	0.5083	0.4632	0.4224	0.3855
11	0.8963	0.8043	0.7224	0.6496	0.5847	0.5268	0.4751	0.4289	0.3875	0.3505
12	0.8874	0.7885	0.7014	0.6246	0.5568	0.4970	0.4440	0.3971	0.3555	0.3186
13	0.8787	0.7730	0.6810	0.6006	0.5303	0.4688	0.4150	0.3677	0.3262	0.2987
14	0.8700	0.7579	0.6611	0.5775	0.5051	0.4423	0.3878	0.3405	0.2992	0.2633
15	0.8613	0.7430	0.6419	0.5553	0.4810	0.4173	0.3624	0.3152	0.2745	0.2394
16	0.8528	0.7284	0.6232	0.5339	0.4581	0.3936	0.3387	0.2919	0.2519	0.2176
17	0.8444	0.7142	0.6050	0.5134	0.4363	0.3714	0.3166	0.2703	0.2311	0.1978
18	0.8360	0.7002	0.5874	0.4936	0.4155	0.3503	0.2959	0.2502	0.2120	0.1799
19	0.8277	0.6864	0.5703	0.4746	0.3957	0.3305	0.2765	0.2317	0.1945	0.1635
20	0.8195	0.6730	0.5537	0.4564	0.3769	0.3118	0.2584	0.2145	0.1784	0.1486
21	0.8114	0.6598	0.5375	0.4388	0.3589	0.2942	0.2415	0.1987	0.1637	0.1351
22	0.8034	0.6468	0.5219	0.4220	0.3418	0.2775	0.2257	0.1839	0.1502	0.1228
23	0.7954	0.6342	0.5067	0.4057	0.3256	0.2618	0.2109	0.1703	0.1378	0.1117
24	0.7876	0.6217	0.4919	0.3901	0.3101	0.2470	0.1971	0.1577	0.1264	0.1015
25	0.7798	0.6095	0.4776	0.3751	0.2953	0.2330	0.1842	0.1460	0.1160	0.0923
26	0.7720	0.5976	0.4637	0.3607	0.2812	0.2198	0.1722	0.1352	0.1064	0.0839
27	0.7644	0.5859	0.4502	0.3468	0.2678	0.2074	0.1609	0.1252	0.0976	0.0763
28	0.7568	0.5744	0.4371	0.3335	0.2552	0.1956	0.1504	0.1159	0.0895	0.0693
29	0.7493	0.5631	0.4243	0.3207	0.2429	0.1846	0.1406	0.1073	0.0822	0.0630
30	0.7419	0.5521	0.4120	0.3083	0.2314	0.1741	0.1314	0.0994	0.0754	0.0573

Year	11%	12%	13%	14%	15%	16%	17%	18%	19%	20%
1	0.9009	0.8929	0.8850	0.8772	0.8696	0.8621	0.8547	0.8475	0.8403	0.8333
2	0.8116	0.7972	0.7831	0.7695	0.7561	0.7432	0.7305	0.7182	0.7062	0.6944
3	0.7312	0.7118	0.6913	0.6750	0.6575	0.6407	0.6244	0.6086	0.5934	0.5787
4	0.6587	0.6355	0.6133	0.5921	0.5718	0.5523	0.5337	0.5158	0.4987	0.4823
5	0.5935	0.5674	0.5428	0.5194	0.4972	0.4761	0.4561	0.4371	0.4190	0.4019
6	0.5346	0.5066	0.4803	0.4556	0.4323	0.4104	0.3898	0.3704	0.3521	0.3349
7	0.4817	0.4523	0.4251	0.3996	0.3759	0.3538	0.3332	0.3139	0.2959	0.2791
8	0.4339	0.4039	0.3762	0.3506	0.3269	0.3050	0.2848	0.2660	0.2487	0.2326
9	0.3909	0.3606	0.3329	0.3075	0.2843	0.2630	0.2434	0.2255	0.2090	0.1938
10	0.3522	0.3220	0.2946	0.2697	0.2472	0.2267	0.2080	0.1911	0.1756	0.1615
11	0.3173	0.2875	0.2607	0.2366	0.2149	0.1954	0.1778	0.1619	0.1476	0.1346
12	0.2858	0.2567	0.2307	0.2076	0.1869	0.1685	0.1520	0.1372	0.1240	0.1122
13	0.2575	0.2292	0.2042	0.1821	0.1625	0.1452	0.1299	0.1163	0.1042	0.0935
14	0.2320	0.2046	0.1807	0.1597	0.1413	0.1252	0.1110	0.0985	0.0876	0.0779
15	0.2090	0.1827	0.1599	0.1401	0.1229	0.1079	0.0949	0.0835	0.0736	0.0649
16	0.1883	0.1631	0.1415	0.1229	0.1069	0.0930	0.0811	0.0708	0.0618	0.0541
17	0.1696	0.1456	0.1252	0.1078	0.0929	0.0802	0.0693	0.0600	0.0520	0.0451
18	0.1528	0.1300	0.1108	0.0946	0.0808	0.0691	0.0592	0.0508	0.0437	0.0376
19	0.1377	0.1161	0.0981	0.0829	0.0703	0.0596	0.0506	0.0431	0.0367	0.0313
20	0.1240	0.1037	0.0868	0.0728	0.0611	0.0514	0.0433	0.0365	0.0308	0.0261
21	0.1117	0.0926	0.0768	0.0638	0.0531	0.0443	0.0370	0.0309	0.0259	0.0217
22	0.1007	0.0826	0.0680	0.0560	0.0462	0.0382	0.0316	0.0262	0.0218	0.0181
23	0.0907	0.0738	0.0601	0.0491	0.0402	0.0329	0.0270	0.0222	0.0183	0.0151
24	0.0817	0.0659	0.0532	0.0431	0.0349	0.0284	0.0231	0.0188	0.0154	0.0126
25	0.0736	0.0588	0.0471	0.0378	0.0304	0.0245	0.0197	0.0160	0.0129	0.0105
26	0.0663	0.0525	0.0417	0.0331	0.0264	0.0211	0.0169	0.0135	0.0109	0.0087
27	0.0597	0.0469	0.0369	0.0291	0.0230	0.0182	0.0144	0.0115	0.0091	0.0073
28	0.0538	0.0419	0.0326	0.0255	0.0200	0.0157	0.0123	0.0097	0.0077	0.0061
29	0.0485	0.0374	0.0289	0.0224	0.0174	0.0135	0.0105	0.0082	0.0064	0.0051
30	0.0437	0.0334	0.0256	0.0196	0.0151	0.0116	0.0090	0.0070	0.0054	0.0042

Year	21%	22%	23%	24%	25%	26%	27%	28%	29%	30%
1	0.8264	0.8197	0.8130	0.8065	0.8000	0.7937	0.7874	0.7813	0.7752	0.7692
2	0.6830	0.6719	0.6610	0.6504	0.6400	0.6299	0.6200	0.6104	0.6009	0.5917
3	0.5645	0.5507	0.5374	0.5245	0.5120	0.4999	0.4882	0.4768	0.4658	0.4552
4	0.4665	0.4514	0.4369	0.4230	0.4096	0.3968	0.3844	0.3725	0.3611	0.3501
5	0.3855	0.3700	0.3552	0.3411	0.3277	0.3149	0.3027	0.2910	0.2799	0.2693
6	0.3186	0.3033	0.2888	0.2751	0.2621	0.2499	0.2383	0.2274	0.2170	0.2072
7	0.2633	0.2486	0.2348	0.2218	0.2097	0.1983	0.1877	0.1776	0.1682	0.1594
8	0.2176	0.2038	0.1909	0.1789	0.1678	0.1574	0.1478	0.1388	0.1304	0.1226
9	0.1799	0.1670	0.1552	0.1443	0.1342	0.1249	0.1164	0.1084	0.1011	0.0943
10	0.1486	0.1369	0.1262	0.1164	0.1074	0.0992	0.0916	0.0847	0.0784	0.0725
11	0.1228	0.1122	0.1026	0.0938	0.0859	0.0787	0.0721	0.0662	0.0607	0.0558
12	0.1015	0.0920	0.0834	0.0757	0.0687	0.0625	0.0568	0.0517	0.0471	0.0429
13	0.0839	0.0754	0.0678	0.0610	0.0550	0.0496	0.0447	0.0404	0.0365	0.0330
14	0.0693	0.0618	0.0551	0.0492	0.0440	0.0393	0.0352	0.0316	0.0283	0.0253
15	0.0573	0.0507	0.0448	0.0397	0.0352	0.0312	0.0277	0.0247	0.0219	0.0195
16	0.0474	0.0415	0.0364	0.0320	0.0281	0.0248	0.0218	0.0193	0.0170	0.0150
17	0.0391	0.0340	0.0296	0.0258	0.0225	0.0197	0.0172	0.0150	0.0132	0.0116
18	0.0323	0.0279	0.0241	0.0208	0.0180	0.0156	0.0135	0.0118	0.0102	0.0089
19	0.0267	0.0229	0.0196	0.0168	0.0144	0.0124	0.0107	0.0092	0.0079	0.0068
20	0.0221	0.0187	0.0159	0.0135	0.0115	0.0098	0.0084	0.0072	0.0061	0.0053
21	0.0183	0.0154	0.0129	0.0109	0.0092	0.0078	0.0066	0.0056	0.0048	0.0040
22	0.0151	0.0126	0.0105	0.0088	0.0074	0.0062	0.0052	0.0044	0.0037	0.0031
23	0.0125	0.0103	0.0086	0.0071	0.0059	0.0049	0.0041	0.0034	0.0029	0.0024
24	0.0103	0.0085	0.0070	0.0057	0.0047	0.0039	0.0032	0.0027	0.0022	0.0018
25	0.0085	0.0069	0.0057	0.0046	0.0038	0.0031	0.0025	0.0021	0.0017	0.0014
26	0.0070	0.0057	0.0046	0.0037	0.0030	0.0025	0.0020	0.0016	0.0013	0.0011
27	0.0058	0.0047	0.0037	0.0030	0.0024	0.0019	0.0016	0.0013	0.0010	0.0008
28	0.0048	0.0038	0.0030	0.0024	0.0019	0.0015	0.0012	0.0010	0.0008	0.0006
29	0.0040	0.0031	0.0025	0.0020	0.0015	0.0012	0.0010	0.0008	0.0006	0.0005
30	0.0033	0.0026	0.0020	0.0016	0.0012	0.0010	0.0008	0.0006	0.0005	0.0004

Index

Other AMACOM books

Accounting Fundamentals for Nonfinancial Executives
Allen Sweeny
"An eye opener...makes basic accounting ideas understandable." *Financial Executive* "...for the manager who finds financial reports about as meaningful as Egyptian hieroglyphics, this book provides a basic step-by-step introduction to the accounting process." *Business Week*   **$10.95**

Budgeting Fundamentals for Nonfinancial Executives
Allen Sweeny and John N. Wisner, Jr.
A Selection of the Macmillan Executive Program Book Club and the Dun & Bradstreet Executive Reader's Service Book Club

"This eight-chapter book contains a clear explanation of all facets of the budget—its control, accounting responsibility, types of costs and their behavior; hitting budget targets and protecting profits—all topics of daily discussion among executives."
The Insurance Salesman   **$12.95**

Cost Accounting Concepts for Nonfinancial Executives
Joseph Peter Simini
"....comprehensive...touches on a surprising number of cost concepts...well written and a useful addition to accounting literature. Simini's straightforward, nontechnical approach will appeal to those executives who are anxious to gain an abbreviated exposure to cost concepts." *The Accounting Review*   **$12.95**

Deskbook of Business Management Terms
Leon A. Wortman
This book puts you in command of the dialects of finance, economics, law, industrial relations, production, insurance, marketing, data processing, and the broad-based vocabulary of general management! "...an invaluable and readily accessible reference tool in all types of organizations."
Los Angeles Journal of Commerce   **$24.95**

A Division of American Management Associations
135 West 50th Street, New York, N.Y. 10020

0-8144-5553-0

658.1527
Sw974

109 356